EVERBLOOMING:

THROUGH THE TWELVE PROVINCES OF THE NETHERLANDS

Ann Marie Ruby

Disclaimer:

This book ("*Everblooming: Through The Twelve Provinces Of The Netherlands*") represents the personal views and opinions of the author ("*Ann Marie Ruby*"). In no way, does it represent or endorse any religious, philosophical, political or scientific view, or any of the stories and individuals mentioned. This book has been written in good faith for people of all cultures and beliefs. It has been written in American English. There may be minor variations in the spelling of names and dates due to translations from Dutch, provincial languages, and regional dialects, or minor discrepancies in historical records.

Although the author and publisher have made efforts to ensure information in this book was correct at publication, they do not assume and hereby disclaim any liability to any party for any loss, damage, or disruption caused by errors, omissions, or any other reason. No guarantee of exact factual accounts of any of the stories is claimed. Stories mentioned have been verified as much as possible; however, stories and accounts may change over time. Along with historical events, this book also includes legends and tales.

As all stories mentioned are readily available online, locally, or within other books, this book is not breaching the privacy of any individual, place, or business. Stories addressing paranormal activity are solely opinions of those who have kept the stories alive. Neither the author nor publisher is supporting claims of paranormal activity in the stories. The intent of this book is to preserve the stories and history of the Netherlands for future generations.

Published in the United States of America, 2020.

ISBN-10: 0-578-74120-2

ISBN-13: 978-0-578-74120-8

DEDICATION

"Today comes and gifts her blessings to all when she dedicates her stories as a guide for the future, for she knows as you the present receive her gift, she is then the past."

-Ann Marie Ruby

Travelers of life we all are yet connected to one another through the pages of life. From time to time, these pages are gathered through the blessed hands of the unknown travelers and bound into books. These books become a part of our life and we keep them as keepsakes for our future generations to become a part of.

This book is one such diary, where I have found people from the past who lived within the same places we live today. Buried within the walls of our homes are the tales of the past inhabitants. Tomorrow, our future generations will reside within this same home you and I call Earth.

Koninkrijk der Nederlanden (English: Kingdom of the Netherlands) includes the Netherlands in Europe, and Aruba, Curaçao and Sint Maarten in the Caribbean. In this book, however, I have only focused on the Netherlands, a small European country sometimes only known for the beautiful fields of tulips. If you have read my previous book, *The Netherlands: Land Of My Dreams*, you know this country is so much more and has contributed so much to this one world. As I had introduced this amazing country to you, my readers, I am blessed to know you had accepted my gift and returned the blessings as you made my book an international number-one bestseller.

So, today I bring to you my family of readers, not the country, but her people – the historical figures from her past. These people had been loved, feared, disgraced, and at times admired by all of us. From their lives, we have some amazing Dutch stories that will become tales read nightly. Faded and lost, they had all become as time separates their stories from us through the door of memories. Yet today, I have gathered some tales from the memory lanes of life.

Some of these stories have been kept alive through various written diaries of the past. Their stories had touched me so much as I had traveled through the twelve provinces of the Netherlands. Some stories came from tour guides, some came from hotel clerks, and some came from complete strangers. After a wide range of traveling and discovering, I was able to gather a handsome number of stories to gift you all through the pages of my book.

I would like to dedicate this book to my future generations. I know time is a blessed path where one day I will have my future generations meet me at the meeting path of life. For them, I live my life in accordance with my basic moral values. Whenever I fall and feel lonely, I find strength from my past generations who are looking down at me from the skies. To move forward, however, I find strength from my future generations.

As a spiritual person, I am single and believe in true twin flames. I keep the lantern of hope glowing for my to-be-found future husband, children, grandchildren, great-grandchildren, and so forth. History is the best teacher of life. For her, we the present learn what to look out for and what we should not repeat. Therefore, from the past of my future generations, I give them the blessed stories of a country I love. With these stories, may they find hope and courage for themselves and their future generations.

Remember, my future generations, this book has gathered only a few tales from the past which I know you all shall read and learn from. I hope you all include your found stories upon this journey of life as you become the present generation. You too, must then retell all the tales that inspire you in the form of a book in the future.

For you, I have found the courage to write today. May we meet tomorrow as time passes by. Until then, I will keep my hope glowing for all of you. For my love of history, the historical figures who inspire and shape us, and for the hope of my own future generations, I dedicate this book to my future generations.

May my love and blessings from the past be with my future generations forever throughout eternity. I have named this book *Everblooming* as I believe all lives on this Earth are everblooming through our memories as we keep them alive throughout time. As the figures in this book are everblooming, so is my love for all of you my future generations. Remember forever, my love for all of you shall always be everblooming.

MESSAGE FROM THE AUTHOR

"Messages received through the time travels of life become epical as they come from the past to the present for the future."

-Ann Marie Ruby

Messages left in a bottle are found floating within the rivers of life. Throughout time, we the humans find ourselves attracted to the past inhabitants through their mysterious, inspirational, and dedicated lives they had lived and left behind. We the present find ourselves uniting with the past and again tie our bonds with the future through the travel journeys of life.

Messages are given like letters from the past, to guide us and be the walking cane for us throughout time. Preserving the messages from the past to guide the future generations became my journey as I began to write this book. I asked myself, how could I from the present time, unite the past, present, and future? The answer came from the lives lived in the past.

As I traveled through a country I call my dreamland, I knew I had to do something for the country I so much love. My love for her had given birth to my bestseller, *The Netherlands: Land Of My Dreams*. Yet, what could I do for her past, present, and future generations?

I admire the past lives that have spoken to me through the buried walls of the past. The future generations need to hear them and learn from them. My fear was, what if these stories get lost in time? Like scattered pages, they become a part of history but not all the pages are available to all.

My tired and exhausted journey through life has taught me words are the most precious gifts one can give and leave behind. When words are converted to tales, they become eternal. My physical journey through the Netherlands has given my inner soul the encouragement and power to awaken and do something for all twelve provinces of the Netherlands.

Within this blessed land, I have traveled by plane, by bus, by tram, by train, by car, by boat, and on foot as I gathered stories from the past lives lived. These are stories as believed by the receivers, and I have taken them to my heart. Afraid for those who lived through the tales I was, as I wondered what if over time, their stories get lost?

I knew I must do something for the past generations of the Netherlands. This land has taken space within my inner love which I know forever shall only grow as my love united with your love for me shall become historical. I wanted the world to know why I love this land. So, I had given my previous book as a gift for the world.

Today, I have historical, romantic, horror, and inspirational stories from the buried walls of the past. Within my book, I have given them a place as I honored their stories to introduce you to them. The bridge of union has been created through my pen and paper as I have brought their stories back to life. Characters of the past are now portraits talking to you through the pages of my book.

Like an artist paints life on the canvas through his or her hands, I have through my words brought the memories of these characters back to life forever within the pages of my book. You, the reader, too have become a part of this journey as you take my hands and travel with me through the twelve provinces of the Netherlands. Throughout time, you can retell these stories to your children as bedtime favorites. These Dutch stories bound together will forever be a keepsake within the homes of all throughout this world.

Some stories you are aware of and some you might not know. Yet, the known and unknown stories have today made it within the pages of my book. These names and their life stories have somehow touched my inner spirit in a different way. I would like you to remember them as you travel to this land. Or, if you are a citizen of this land, then do know they too had a home within this blessed land before you. Today, they are the past inhabitants.

For the admired Father of the Fatherland, William the Silent, I had dedicated a chapter within my previous book as I am his admirer. I know some famous names are always within the portraits of your homes such as the beloved painters Johannes Vermeer, Rembrandt Harmenszoon van Rijn, Vincent Willem van Gogh, and so many known or unknown names. I too am inspired by them, however, I could only select a few names from my travel diaries within the Netherlands.

These past inhabitants, through their life stories, have come alive within this book and shall guide you to be a better person. Turn the pages and learn from the past. Live within the present as you learn from their lives lived. Send messages off to your future generations as you sign and leave behind this keepsake book for your future generations. May these amazing life stories be there for you the present, and as a lesson from the past to guide your future.

My message to the world today is, let us in union learn from the past. My love for this land has now given birth to another book gathered through the lives lived of her past generations. May this book be my gift to the past, present, and future generations.

The future is bright, and we shall be a better world as we unite the past, present, and future through the pages of a book. Dear all, from my love for a country I call my dreamland, I have woven this book of stories. Within these pages, the past generations guide us the present and you the future as I retell through my words, the stories of the past.

Through time, some stories and facts change, for which I wanted to preserve these stories. I have tried to keep them as accurate as possible. Within these pages, I have placed my favorite stories for the world citizens to share and keep as a storyteller for all times. I give you with love and blessings:

EVERBLOOMING:
THROUGH THE TWELVE PROVINCES
OF THE NETHERLANDS

TABLE OF CONTENTS

INTRODUCTION

"Memories of the past gather upon pages and become a diary, yet when introduced to the world, they become a book."

-Ann Marie Ruby

The Netherlands

THE NETHERLANDS

Dawn breaks through

As the morning sun reaches this land.

The North Sea sings her sweet song of peace

As she kisses this land.

Hope finds love and blooms

As the singing tulips on this land.

The windmills join in this loving performance of nature,

As they send the rejuvenating music

Floating within this land.

Humans catch a glimpse of nature's musical recital

As they too want to participate in nature's true concert

Across this musical land.

The inhabitants of this land awaken to the sound

Of the harmonious musical tunes upon this land.

The water, the land, and the air,

Find travelers knocking, seeking, and asking

For the identity of this land.

The seeking travelers find peace

As they enter this majestic land.

Embracing all her citizens and travelers,

Love blossoms within this land.

She smiles back at her children and guests,

As she welcomes all to rejuvenate in the water of her land.

She sings her sweet musical tunes

Through the windmills of her land.

She presents a musical concert for all to remember her by

As her children and guests know at dawn, they all awaken,

And at dusk, they all go to sleep,

Yet all the travelers have this day to fill up their jug

Of memories and spread them throughout this land.

Remember, the musical concert of this day

Continues throughout time as the memories are kept alive

Throughout this land.

As a keepsake throughout time,

Within the hands of all is given a love letter which reads,

Forget me not,

For you,

I am

THE NETHERLANDS.

Scattered pages filled with emotional stories arrived upon my hands. Tearful romance stories we hear of when they are not happily ever after. Horror stories are buried within the walls that haunted the past and still haunt the present. Historical stories are left behind to teach all and create a bridge uniting the past, present, and future.

Voices from the past live on throughout time through the words of their beholders. Educational messages travel time as we the present complete the blessed work the past inhabitants had started. The stories change as the listeners recall to the best of their knowledge.

I wished for a sacred chest that would hold all the stories safely within her for all generations to come. These stories should not be lost to the future but saved by the hands of the present for the future. This chest would be made out of love. To open this chest, all one needs to do is turn the pages. Yes, I found my sacred chest as I bound the scattered pages of the past containing amazing stories.

These narratives were found and collected as I the traveler sought them through the twelve provinces of the Netherlands. My hands gathered them upon the pages of my diaries as I placed pen to paper. Letters from the chest of the past knocked upon my door as I opened and accepted them within my inner chest. Memories of the past now take life as they are given a place within the pages of my book.

For you today, for your children tomorrow, and your grandchildren in the near future, to keep as a keepsake, I give you my blessed gift. I call her:

Everblooming:
Through The Twelve Provinces
Of The Netherlands.

CHAPTER ONE:

NOORD-HOLLAND

"From creating traditional clothing to framing your landscape with the blooming tulips and singing windmills, you have been framed within the canvases of this world."

-Ann Marie Ruby

Noord-Holland

NOORD-HOLLAND

My path is complete

As I am blessed with this world's peaceful visitors.

I am home to Amsterdam, the capital city

Of this low-lying country,

Known to you as the Netherlands.

I have the heavenly colors within my chest

Which bring sparkles of joy to all

As you call my gardens, the garden of Europe.

I kiss your memories

As you remember me through my tulips.

We can all gather for a story night in my Dam Square

And listen to tales of my past inhabitants.

I love listening to all different languages spoken

By my visitors, as I teach you mine and treasure yours too.

My capital city is Haarlem.

Do stop by my shore, as I am known in the Netherlands

As the province

NOORD-HOLLAND.

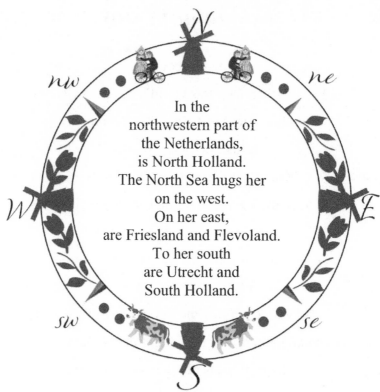

In the
northwestern part of
the Netherlands,
is North Holland.
The North Sea hugs her
on the west.
On her east,
are Friesland and Flevoland.
To her south
are Utrecht and
South Holland.

Welcome to Noord-Holland (English: North Holland). The capital of this province is Haarlem. The Noordzee (English: North Sea) splashes her salty water upon the shores of one of the most famous provinces as seen within the eyes of the visitors. She keeps the memories of her past children alive within her deep sea as she spreads the memories around the globe. North Holland is a province known for her beauty and nature. Travelers from all around the globe are attracted to this land as this is a haven for global tourists. Twin flames are found kissing upon the Magere

Brug (English: Skinny Bridge), strolling through the heavenly tulip fields, or walking in Dam Square.

The capital of the Netherlands, Amsterdam, is found within North Holland. Enter this magical city through Amsterdam Airport Schiphol, which in 2020 was voted the number one best airport in western Europe and amongst the top ten in the world by passengers at the Skytrax World Airport Awards. The name Schiphol has numerous tales about its origin. One such tale refers to its English meaning, "Ships Hell" because the airport is located on what used to be the Haarlemmermeer (English: Haarlem's lake), where many ships were lost due to catastrophic storms. The lake was drained, and land was reclaimed from below to build the polder of Haarlemmermeer where the airport now sits.

As you leave the airport to start your journey through North Holland, get on a rickshaw and see Amsterdam, through different eyes. This city is also known as the Venice of the North for its various canals must be traveled through the water. North Holland is also home to three UNESCO World Heritage Sites. Do remember to visit the Droogmakerij de Beemster (English: Beemster Polder), Defence Line of Amsterdam, and the Seventeenth-Century Canal Ring Area of Amsterdam inside the Singelgracht.

Upon your next visit to North Holland, do take this book along and remember the stories of the past inhabitants. Like you walk today, they too were walking upon the same ground once upon a time. The bridge separating you from them is time and space.

Yet, today I want you the visitors to hold on to your seats as I take you on a tour through the personal life stories of some of the past inhabitants of North Holland.

HELENA'S ENVY

Amsterdam finds her tourists from all over the world. Famous people are known to wine and dine within the nation's capital. As you walk through the streets of Amsterdam, do get acquainted with a person known as Helena.

She lived on Spooksteeg (English: Ghost Alley), the oldest part within the Red Light District of Amsterdam. She lived there with her father who was a tanner, and her sister Dina, during the eighteenth century. Both sisters were incredibly beautiful.

A sailor had fallen in love with Dina. As a soft-hearted and kind soul, Dina too fell in love with the sailor. The sailor would send a lot of love letters to Dina, but Helena out of envy and jealousy had always burned them before Dina could get them. As Dina found out the truth, however, it was then her love story faced a fatal twist.

Dina's love story did not last long as it fell upon the evil eyes of her sister Helena. Overcome by her jealousy, envy, and lust, Helena committed the unthinkable deadly sin. Helena pushed her sister Dina into the cellar of their father's tannery and killed her. The local residents had concluded the incident after discovering the body, to be a fatal accident.

After committing this horrendous crime, Helena went and married her sister's beloved sailor. In 1753, as Helena laid on her sickbed dying, she confessed her sin to the sailor. The dying person's confession went unheard and was left unforgiven as her husband refused to forgive this sin.

Helena's husband out of his love for his lost beloved Dina, had cursed Helena. He cursed Helena to be forever miserable stating, "Wees verdoemd, zustermoordenares, je zult ronddolen op de plaats van je misdaad tot in eeuwigheid." This translates to English as, "Be damned, sister murderer, you will roam the scene of your crime forever."

Perhaps he could not give Helena another chance as Helena never gave her sister Dina another chance in life. God forgives sins, even those unforgiveable by humans. Yet, even a century after Helena's death, it is said that screams could be heard at the crime site.

People have reported witnessing an incredibly distorted and screaming woman seeking forgiveness within the dark alleys. Peace finds herself as the seeker seeks

14

forgiveness. Helena never found peace as her envy deprived Dina of her love and life. Envy is a deadly sin as within the Abrahamic books, this sin was committed by Cain. There, we had brother against brother, where Cain had taken Abel's life out of envy.

Today, as you visit Amsterdam, do remember you may see and hear Helena still roaming around, trying to find forgiveness and peace. As no one can separate twin flames, the sailor's love for Dina, from the Netherlands, shall be everblooming.

ANNE FRANK'S GROTTO

Annelies Marie "Anne" Frank, the famous diarist was born on June 12, 1929 in Frankfurt, Germany. Her parents were Edith Frank and Otto Heinrich Frank. She also had an older sister by the name of Margot Frank. The Frank family was a liberal Jewish family.

To escape Adolf Hitler and his Nazi party's catastrophic brutality, the Frank family had to move back and forth between places to find a secure area to live in. They were not spared from the brutality of the past racial discriminations. A granted homeland, we call the specific part of Earth we are born in. Yet, it is the mighty racial discriminators who take the power of their voice and decide the fate of their victims.

Deprived of their homes and homeland, the victims travel around the Earth only to be accepted by another land and place. Escaping the brutal door of death, over 300,000 Jews had fled Germany from the year 1933 to 1939. The Frank family was one such family who had finally united in Amsterdam, the Netherlands.

The unfaithful fate, however, had come to hunt this family even when the family had tried to run away from it. The Frank family had hidden in what is now called the Anne Frank House, at Prinsengracht 263 in Amsterdam. They took shelter in this building as there was an annex at the back that was not visible from the outside. They used a bookcase to block the annex they hid themselves within.

They lived in this shelter for two years during World War II. With the Frank family, there were four other Jews who also hid in the annex. The famous diary that so many children and adults throughout this world either have read or will read was created here by a child. Anne Frank's daily notations were her gift for all generations to come. She had wanted to publish this diary as a book if she were to survive.

The Frank family, however, after being betrayed had their annex invaded. To this day, no one is sure who the betrayer was. The Frank family ended up at the Westerbork transit camp in the province of Drenthe. Then, they were deported to the Auschwitz concentration camp in Poland. The sisters were taken to Bergen-Belsen in Germany. In 1945, Otto Frank had found himself the sole survivor of his family, as Auschwitz was eventually liberated.

Hermine "Miep" Gies used to work for Otto Frank in Amsterdam and was one of the courageous people who even at the risk of her own life tried to keep the Frank family safe in the annex. Even after the refugees in the annex were caught, Gies kept Anne Frank's diaries and papers safe. For this, Otto Frank was able to gift his daughter's diaries to the future.

The Anne Frank House in Amsterdam is rumored to be haunted as reported by her visitors and employees. There are numerous accounts of seeing a girl watching through the windows and standing at the windows. Sounds are also heard on the staircase in the annex behind where the bookcase was. People have reported cold spots in the house. Some feel like they are being watched. Even with the cold feeling of being haunted, this place is a miracle as we have the amazing girl's diary from here.

The Anne Frank House stands as the writer's house. This is a museum dedicated to a great writer who wanted to be an author. This house is a symbol of freedom, even after death. Not even death could prevent Anne Frank from becoming an author.

Her stories were a gift to the world and are within the hands of all whom love her even to this day. She will through her words of wisdom, guide all who pick up her diary. Anne Frank will through the pages of her diary, from the Netherlands, be everblooming.

HET SPINHUIS AND THE FORBIDDEN LOVE

Walking through Dam Square are all the locals and tourists who visit North Holland. A short walk through Dam Square will bring the tourists to Het Spinhuis (English: The Spin House) located at Oudezijds Achterburgwal 185 in Amsterdam. Today, this building houses the Meertens Institute and the Huygens Institute for Dutch History.

Let us walk back in time to 1597, when this house had been used as a penitentiary for women. The detention center was used to punish women convicted of petty or larger crimes, such as begging, adultery, thievery, or drinking. The criminals who had committed petty crimes were kept separate from those who had bigger crimes on their hands. The reasoning was to correct and bring all women back to society safely. It is said they were asked to read the Bible to help themselves. The women had spent their days sewing and spinning so they could be useful to the society and teach themselves handicrafts.

Although ownership of the building has changed over time, the building is said to have a dark secret hidden within her walls. If only the walls could speak of the former residents, they would talk about a forbidden love story buried within them. A young woman had arrived there to serve her punishment. One day, she had done the unthinkable as she had fallen in love with a priest. He too committed the sin of falling in love with this woman. Like so many love stories that come upon our doors that are only those of sad endings, this too ended up as a tragedy.

The woman was punished because of their attraction toward one another. She was punished to spend the rest of her days sewing garments as did most of the residents. As priests were not allowed to marry, he committed suicide because he blamed himself for her punishment. It is said that even to this day where the priest took his life, the hotel employees hear and see the priest's ghost. Some even say his ghost is visible in a particular room.

Years later, in 1805, Maria Aletta Hulshoff was also punished and imprisoned there for two years. Her crime was that she had opposed the arrival of Louis Napoleon Bonaparte. When visiting this site, do remember these stories and all whom had been sentenced here.

Love is immortal, even though life is mortal. Some might judge the actions of the lovers or some might say it is the reaction of the earthly punishers. We the world citizens have over and over again tried to separate true love by forcing religious, social, or political differences upon them. Sometimes, these differences were immense, and they lost to our forceful ways of wrongful results.

I ask you why would you want to separate true love? Think about your actions. Society judges before placing oneself in the position. How could you place yourself in another person's shoes? The shoes will never fit as they were only made for that person. Then, how is it you become the judge? My conclusion is let the judged not be the judge. Sometimes, it does not matter who is wrong or who is right. The wrongful and powerful voices of the wrong are always loud and have wronged historically.

They shall wrong eternally unless we wake up and let true twin flames make their own decision even if this is wrong within the eyes of this world. Let them be wrong or let them be right. But at least let them unite for one another. Let us not be the obstacle. Let us be the observer from afar as twin flames unite, or separate as they choose, for they are like this couple from the Netherlands, everblooming.

CHAPTER TWO:

ZUID-HOLLAND

"All seek peace, yet peace has found herself a home within you, known as the Peace Palace."

-Ann Marie Ruby

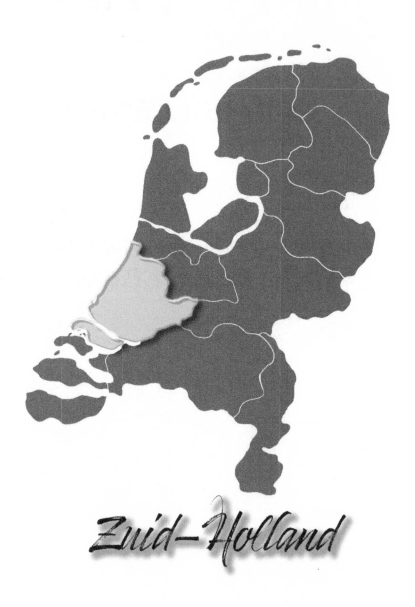

Zuid-Holland

ZUID-HOLLAND

The flying wings of peace found her home here.

Peace accepted all of you as you have accepted peace.

Peace finds a home within the seekers of her.

The blessed North Sea too has found peace within this land

As the citizens have made peace with her.

My shores have seen so many ships sail throughout time,

As I have Europe's largest seaport.

I have given a home to all the politicians as

My capital city Den Haag

Is also the political capital of my country.

Within my chest, you will find the founding fathers

And the royal family as I have kept them sacredly

In history for all of you to learn from

As I know history is the world's best teacher.

From Gouda cheese,

To Delft pottery,

To the healing waters of Scheveningen,

I entertain you all within my chest.

For all of you, I am known as the province

With the most inhabitants in the Netherlands.

Today, I welcome all of you to my land,

To find peace, justice, and harmony,

To be in peace and learn peace as I house the Vredespaleis,

Where you can wish upon a tree.

In my country, the Netherlands, I am known

As the province

ZUID-HOLLAND.

In the
western part of
the Netherlands,
is South Holland.
The North Sea hugs her
on the west.
On her east,
are Utrecht and Gelderland.
To her north, is North Holland.
To her south, are Zeeland
and North Brabant.

Welcome to Zuid-Holland (English: South Holland). The capital of this province is Den Haag (English: The Hague). Even though Amsterdam in North Holland is the nation's capital, The Hague in the province of South Holland is the nation's political capital. Here, all of the Dutch political leaders gather in the oldest gothic castle and parliamentary building still in use to this day, the Binnenhof (English: Inner Court).

The Royal Palace, Huis Ten Bosch (English: House in the Woods) is also in The Hague. It is one of the three

27

official royal residences where His Majesty, King Willem-Alexander Claus George Ferdinand, and his consort, Her Majesty Queen Máxima Zorreguieta Cerruti, reside with their three daughters. His Majesty has reigned since his mother, the former Queen Beatrix's abdication in 2013.

The current Prime Minster of the Netherlands is Mark Rutte (VVD). He has been the elected Prime Minister since October 14, 2010. The Netherlands got their first liberal Prime Minister in ninety-two years with the victory of Prime Minister Mark Rutte.

As of 2020, he has been in this position for the last ten years as the population love him and have re-elected him over and over again. He is known as the son of The Hague. I call him a human with humanity and have written in my previous books about how I admire him as a great human being.

The Hague which is also known as home of the Vredespaleis (English: Peace Palace), is my personal favorite place on the entire Earth. As a traveler, I have traveled around the globe, but I found my inner peace as I stood on the dunes near the North Sea in The Hague. This province is also home to two of the UNESCO World Heritage Sites, the Mill Network at Kinderdijk-Elshout and the Van Nellefabriek (English: Van Nelle Factory). Did you know that archaeologists have said South Holland has actually been inhabited for around 7,500 years?

I wonder how people during the olden days had lived their lives. I do not know how they had lived, but today I want to introduce you to some of the previous inhabitants of South Holland.

FATE OF DE WITT BROTHERS

The Binnenhof, where the current elected politicians sit, was still in use when Johan de Witt was elected the Grand Pensionary in 1653. At the time, the Grand Pensionary was what a Prime Minister is today, the political leader. During the famous Dutch Golden Age, Johan de Witt was the head of government until his resignation which was followed by his gruesome death in 1672. He had studied at Leiden University and worked as a lawyer in a law firm. He was married to Wendela Bicker and they had three daughters and one son.

Johan de Witt had his worst days as downfall came to him in 1672. This year is known as the Rampjaar (English: Disaster Year) in Dutch history. William III of Orange had the Dutch citizens' support. During the summer of 1672, Johan de Witt and his older brother Cornelis de Witt resigned from their jobs. Both brothers were facing political demise. A charge was brought against Cornelis de Witt, accusing him of conspiracy to assassinate William III of Orange. There was no proof, but Cornelis de Witt was arrested and held at the Gevangenpoort (English: Prison Gate), only a few minutes' walk from the Binnenhof.

Johan de Witt had gone to visit his brother at the prison. When he went, a group of people there gruesomely attacked Johan and Cornelis de Witt. They were both killed and left there naked, for all local people to do as they pleased. It is said the locals had taken their livers and body parts out, roasted them, and had them like cannibals.

This gruesome historical event still gives chills to the current-day visitors. Today, the prison that once held Cornelis de Witt is now a museum. Museum de Gevangenpoort (English: the Prison Gate Museum) is visited by tourists and is known to be one of the top haunted places in The Hague. Tourists are advised not to visit if you are weak in heart. A statue honoring the politician Johan de Witt stands in The Hague, where the lynching and murder had taken place at the Buitenhof (English: Outer Court). This statue was unveiled to the public on June 12, 1918 by Her Majesty Queen Wilhelmina.

Politicians are elected officials who are chosen. Time and tide might, however, place a river of differences between you and the person in office. The difference of opinion is there to be celebrated as differences generate great ideas which create a bridge of union between the different thoughts. Agreeing to disagree creates the best of friendships where no one gets hurt.

When injustice takes place because of blind love, blind faith, or unjust anger, it is then we learn from history and the historical figures. Knowledge is the peaceful blessing we the humans can get only from the traveling path of history. Let us not erase history but keep history in the pages of the books to learn from.

Just like the de Witt brothers, politicians are elected officials who we the citizens elect. It happens as time goes on, we reject them. We should always remember whatever happens between a politician and the voters are historical lessons. So, history cannot be rejected even if the person is, for history teaches all throughout time. For this reason, Johan de Witt and Cornelis de Witt from the Netherlands will always be everblooming.

WAITING BY THE SEA: THE FISHERMAN'S WIFE

Scheveningen, a district in The Hague, sits by the North Sea. Here, the sand and water kiss as the waves come splashing on the shores. Dawn peeks through the sky upon the North Sea, leaving all residents with days full of hope.

Artists sit upon the shores trying to catch a glimpse of this magnificent beauty on their canvases. Musicians sing and dance with the waves as they gift this world new songs. The sun also sets upon the sea as some go back home to be with their beloved through the night and celebrate yet another dawn in union.

Walk with me on the beautiful shore of the Scheveningen beach as we go and visit a resident from the past. She had once walked on the same shore we the present stand upon. Although we can still sense her today, time separates us from touching her.

There was once upon a time a fisherman's wife who dressed in traditional attire. She stood waiting for her beloved. The story says her beloved husband had gone off to sea and had perished.

She represents the wives of many fishermen who had gone off to the sea and passed away. Scheveningen was known as a fishermen's village. Many residents were also World War II victims, whose ships went missing and had not come back. Were they victims of war or the sea who gives and takes at the same time? While the North Sea shapes the lives of the Dutch, the Dutch have also had their war with the water.

The Oude Kerk (English: Old Church) in Scheveningen has an annual tribute for those who perished at sea. After a blessed service, people walk to the statue of the devoted Vissersvrouw (English: Fisherman's Wife). There on the statue is a poem which depicts a mother, a wife, a person who is longing for her family member or beloved to return. The poem in Dutch is as follows:

"DE ZEE, DIE STEEDS WEER NAM
ZAL EENMAAL WEDERGEVEN
ALLEN DIE ZIJN GEBLEVEN
AAN HEM DIE EERST ONTKWAM
DE HEER VAN WIND EN WATER
AAN CHRISTUS TRIOMFATOR."

This poem translated to English is as follows:

"THE SEA, WHICH TOOK OVER AND OVER AGAIN
WILL ONE DAY GIVE BACK
ALL WHO REMAINED

TO HIM WHO FIRST ESCAPED
THE LORD OF WIND AND WATER
TO CHRIST THE TRIUMPHATOR."

A statue from the past still restores faith in all of us, as she teaches all to never give up on love. Although we the humans are mortal, love is eternal and love is immortal. Even when all is lost and nothing is found, love is found. A fisherman's wife has proven from the past, her love survives time. As the immortal statue in her honor stands on the Scheveningen beach watching over all the fishermen and their wives today, we know within our hearts, this fisherman's wife from the Netherlands shall be everblooming.

JACOB PRONK'S BELIEF IN THE NORTH SEA

The North Sea flows by the Netherlands, Great Britain, Denmark, Norway, Germany, Belgium, and France. She meets Scheveningen as she flows along the western part of the Netherlands. The Dutch are familiar with the furies of the North Sea. They are also remarkably familiar with the love and tender care this sea has shown them. As we enjoy this amazing Scheveningen beach, let us walk back to 1811.

Jacob Pronk, a shipowner, had heard about the healing powers of the North Sea, the seawater, and the fresh sea air. In 1811, Pronk proposed to build a bathhouse on the shore of Scheveningen. Even though the local municipality realized the power of the healing waters, they rejected his ideas. His proposal fell to deaf ears as his fight continued for years. Finally in 1818, he was given permission as he then bought his blessed land on the dunes of Scheveningen.

Near the North Sea, he was finally allowed to build his wooden structure where he had tubs for people to fill up with seawater and bathe. Pronk then provided people with carriages for bathing. He realized people had come from all around as the seawater had healed people who were suffering from rheumatic and nerve diseases. For all the visitors, Pronk eventually built a stone structure in the place of the wooden structure he had before.

His gift given to this world still exists after his death. The Kurhaus hotel was built on the same place of the original bathhouse. Kurhaus in English translates to cure house or health resort, perhaps to honor the original intention for which the bathhouse was built. The original Kurhaus had burned down very soon after it was built. Then, the second Kurhaus was built in its place. This building still stands as a seaside resort. To this day, the amazing hotel continues to host guests.

Believe in yourself and know all good intentions are rewarded. Pronk's efforts were rewarded by the answered prayers of the healed and watching people find comfort for a while. Pronk and his faith had eventually found the path he sought as faith is believing in your quest, not giving up. Today, when you visit Scheveningen, you will still see the Kurhaus standing there as the Grand Hotel Amrâth Kurhaus, reminding all travelers of life that a man's dream today through time became a reality. There is a plaque there that honors Pronk as the founder of the seaside resort in Scheveningen.

Visionaries with their visions create the future. The past, present, and future are united through the journey of a visionary. Here, the Kurhaus is proof of one man's vision. For his vision, Jacob Pronk from the Netherlands shall remain everblooming.

THE WILL OF SKIPPER ARIE EVEGROEN

Nieuwerkerk aan den IJssel is a town in the western Netherlands, in the province of South Holland. The largest seaport of Europe, Port of Rotterdam, is extremely close to this destination, which brings more visitors to the area. Today, as you walk through this area, you would wonder about the past residents and their footprints.

Some people throughout time enter this Earth and leave permanent footprints for all of us to follow. Come travel with me and get to know one such honorable man as we travel not too far back, but only a few years to a devastating cold winter night. Let us travel time to the night of January 31 to February 1, 1953 that will be remembered throughout the Dutch history books for the devastating North Sea flood of 1953.

In the Netherlands, severe wind, high tide, and low pressure all caused the North Sea to rise up to around 14.93 feet (4.55 meters) above sea level. This catastrophic storm had taken nearly two thousand people and thousands of farm animals. Thousands of homes and farms were damaged or destroyed.

During any catastrophe, we the humans face devastation and disaster which in retrospect, blind our thinking ability. At times we freeze in place as to which way we should go, what we should do, and how. During these times, we do have amongst us heroes who awaken and rise above and beyond.

A skipper named Arie Evegroen is one such hero. On a very cold and chilly night, the mayor of Nieuwerkerk aan den IJssel, Jacob Cornelis "Jaap" Vogelaar, had asked Evegroen to go with his grain barge to cover a large hole in the dike of the river IJssel. Cornelis Heuvelman volunteered to help. The mayor had then also asked Johannes Aart van Vliet for his assistance.

These brave humans had gone out of their way to save their fellow humans. These human efforts to save their land from the hungry North Sea, did go unnoticed as do so many true stories. This story is similar to the fictional story of a Dutch boy who had saved his land from floodwaters by keeping his finger on a hole in a dike.

This, however, was a real story of a few Dutch heroes who did not fear for their own lives but went out to save others on a cold winter night. More than fifty years after the event, in addition to Evegroen, the other heroes from that chilly night also received recognition. It is not recognition that creates a hero, but rather the actions taken during catastrophic events create heroes.

Recognizing these humans, however, gives us the humans hope and revitalizes our faith in humans and humanity. Let us all in union regain our faith and belief in humanity. The Dutch citizens are traveling all around the world to teach their human brothers and sisters the methods and ways to deal with devastating floodwaters.

They have reclaimed their lands from floodwaters and rising seawater. Now with experience within their hands, they travel to give you their helping hands. Do welcome their lessons and become a teacher for the future.

My belief is that even within a dark and stormy night, we have skippers like Evegroen sailing the sea with a lantern in his hand to give you the human a helping hand. From the past, a great human traveler of life has turned on his lantern of hope for humanity. Accept his lantern of hope and do keep this glowing as you travel to the future for our past inhabitants teach us through their lessons of life what we are to teach our future generations.

Remember him as you travel and know from the past, Evegroen still glows and teaches as you keep going forward with his messages. For this reason, the skipper Arie Evegroen with his faith and humanity from the Netherlands shall be everblooming.

CHAPTER THREE:

ZEELAND

*"You are home to where the sea
and land meet. For this reason, we
the lovers of sea find ourselves
upon your land."*

-Ann Marie Ruby

ZEELAND

I welcome all of you to my land.

Most of you call me, the land in the sea,

For I have the most waters within this country.

My chest forever keeps the memories

Of the flood victims and my past inhabitants alive.

You can visit and learn about them

As my present inhabitants will recite their stories to you,

Upon the sandy beaches under the night skies.

You will still find Goddess Nehalennia from the past

Watching over all the sailors arriving to

And departing from my shores.

From my shores had taken birth Willem Beuckelszoon,

A Dutch national hero, who taught my inhabitants

How to preserve our most famous food, herring.

My capital city is Middelburg.

Do come and visit me like the flying birds.

I am known within my country, the Netherlands,

As the province

ZEELAND.

In the
southwestern part of
the Netherlands,
is Zeeland.
The North Sea hugs her
on the west.
On her east,
is North Brabant.
To her north,
is South Holland.

Welcome to Zeeland, also spelled historically in English as Zealand. The capital of this province is Middelburg. Zeeland, with her islands and peninsulas, means "sea land" as much of the province was reclaimed from the sea. This province, along with Flevoland as mentioned in a later chapter, is known to have one of the Seven Wonders of the Modern World. The Delta Works consist of human-made structures that were built to prevent another catastrophe like the North Sea flood of 1953.

This flood had taken a big toll on this province, but the Dutch are resilient. They proved they could build back. While keeping the memories, they moved forward. Oosterscheldekering (English: Eastern Scheldt Storm Surge Barrier) as the Dutch call it, is part of the Delta Works, and is the biggest storm surge barrier in the world.

Zeeland is famous for being a major tourist site. This province is also known for her farmland, farm animals, and beaches. The country New Zealand was named after this province. Come and take a trip with me within this amazing province. Let us go back in time and visit the past inhabitants of this land.

MIRACLES OF
THE VROUWEPUTJE

Water quenches thirst. She washes off emotional pain as she flows out of our eyes. She also heals physical pain as she rejuvenates through faith and belief. From the present, where we the world citizens seek a miracle healing well of water, let us travel to the medieval times.

Travel with me to a remote place within the province of Zeeland, to a medieval place of pilgrimage, to where the believers of spirituality had traveled. This place still exists. Within the bridge of time, the faces of the believers have changed, but not their belief.

Dreams from the beyond had awakened a person named Greet. On a dark cold night, she had a visit from the beyond. The visitor is well known to you today as she was worshipped by her host, Greet. This visitor had asked Greet to use the water from a pond to heal people. Greet was asked to give suffering people some help they so needed. This visitor of the night was the Virgin Mary, the mother so many of us worship. This pond is known as the Vrouweputje (English: Women's Well).

The legend continues as it says a woman had used this pond water to heal her arthritic legs. She would have her son bring her the water every day. Once he could not bring it for her and he replaced it with normal water pretending it to be the healing water. The woman, however, immediately knew it was not water from the Vrouweputje.

The medieval Vrouweputje was on its way to becoming extinct as with time, people lose their faith and belief. Local residents and local politicians placed helping hands to save the history. They jumped in to save this natural site and found their victory.

This victory was not only for the belief in the miracle healing water of the Vrouweputje, but also to protect the home of indigenous plants, animals, and much more. A spiritual person or an environmentalist, we all walk for peace and serenity. The united efforts of all sacred individuals combined saved the spiritual belief in the healing water from being demolished.

Maybe you do not believe in miracles or the healing power of the Vrouweputje but believe in the historical natural sites, and the power of humans who work unitedly to save one another and their land. The natural reserve is being taken care of by people who do believe. To believe or not is an individual's choice, yet water heals us now as it did within times past.

The bridge that unites all of us the humans through the years is faith. Through the journey of some travelers, this blessed pond has come back to life. With it, the believers who had been healed in the past too have come back with their stories. They remind us faith is believing, not questioning.

With faith and belief, this pond existed in the past. Through the hard work of some present-day dwellers, it has again come back to life not only to keep the pond everblooming, but with it, the original believers, the present-day believers, and the future believers. They, through their faith, belief, and love of a natural pond, from the Netherlands, shall be everblooming.

GODDESS NEHALENNIA RETURNS

Zeeland has always been a traveler's destination, be it for business or pleasure. She had greeted international visitors who had landed upon her shore years ago and continues to greet the visitors today. What if we could go back in time and find some evidence of these past travelers? Come with me as I take you to one such place where once there were two temples dedicated to a Goddess known as Nehalennia.

During the second and third centuries, fishermen and merchants would stop by Domburg and Ganuenta. They paid their respect to a Celtic or Germanic Goddess, Goddess Nehalennia. The travelers would burn candles and incense for a safe journey through the rough North Sea. The rough sea had eventually buried the temples under the water.

In 1647, the remains of a temple and huge altars were uncovered after a storm hit during the dark night in Domburg. The washed up remains were stored in a church. The church, however, was hit by lightning and burned down. Some artifacts survived. On April 14, 1970, K.J. Bout, a fisherman, had found the sacred stones of another temple near Colijnsplaat in his fishing net. It was discovered there was another temple dedicated to Goddess Nehalennia in what was Ganuenta near Colijnsplaat. As the ancient temple had gone under water, a replica has been built, called the Temple of Nehalennia.

From her permanent residence in Colijnsplaat, this replica temple stands in Zeeland reminding the world that the Netherlands includes all humans with humanity. This is not solely a religious ground, but history revived through the love and honor of all history lovers. I would compare this temple to a woman who stands and watches over her children over the North Sea. People do visit this temple and enjoy the historical significance. There are candles and incense for all who want to place in a prayer for all the children of today, tomorrow, and the past.

Life is a blessing. All prayers said do get an answer through the pages of history when and where there is faith and belief. When visiting, do remember how the stones and prayer altars were discovered is a miracle from the beyond. Like the local pilgrims, you too can visit this sacred temple of the Zeeland Goddess.

Faith in a specific religion or just spirituality matters not, for what matters is the past inhabitants lived on this

Earth we the present live on and even after our time, the future inhabitants will reside here. What ties us in a bond are the findings that prove the existence of the past inhabitants. Through these findings, we are also tied to the future inhabitants.

In the past, there were people who believed in the Goddess, yet the people who found the ancient artifacts believed it or not, helped rebuild the temple. Now, we the present and the future can all visit a temple that is dedicated to a Goddess who watches the land and the water. Through her story, and how the inhabitants of this land saved this temple, Goddess Nehalennia from the Netherlands shall be everblooming.

MIRACLE OF UNITY AT COLIJNSPLAAT

Zeeland has had her share of war and love stories with the North Sea. The rough sea gives and takes as the Dutch citizens have befriended her and learned to live with her. The experiences throughout the years have now made better human beings for the whole world. What we the humans could do when united, is a question placed upon all humans. The answer today again comes to us through the pages of history.

Sometimes, we honor one person for his or her contribution to the society. At times, it is the human effort as a group that prevails. Let us in union travel through a beautiful historical example of humanity within the seafront tourist destination known to you and me as Zeeland.

On the chilling winter night of January 31 through February 1, the devastating flood of 1953 had hit the Netherlands. Thousands of lives, properties, and livestock were lost to this catastrophic devastation. I want all of you to now see another side of this flood where we found within ourselves humanity at its best.

On the disastrous night of 1953, the North Sea had given in all her fury and declared war with the citizens. Colijnsplaat came under the threat of perishing completely as the floodwall was collapsing. It is said that some of the residents went out in force and stood shoulder to shoulder, all for one and one for all. They did not allow the fear of death or physical pain to set them apart.

The force of the mighty water against the human will to save all humans, land, and livestock became larger than any individual life. Their efforts were heard and rewarded as a ship was thrown their way against the weakened floodwall, preventing the floodwater from coming through. The village was spared and to this day, some say the ship came as a miracle. Some say they do not know how the ship came or maybe it was in the right place at the right time. I believe in miracles from the beyond.

On August 6, 1993, the monument "Houen Jongens" was unveiled in Colijnsplaat. The monument shows a large hand, a large wave, and a floodwall. It is a symbol showing humans with their hands united can stop the ravishing floodwaters. This monument is a tribute given to the residents who had fought the great flood of 1953.

This incident is evidence of the human spirit and unity. I know humans united for one another is one of the biggest wonders. Human willpower to save one and all, won on that disastrous night. This is a lesson that shall remain standing on the grounds of Zeeland for this world to witness. This story is not of a person, but the strength of humans united.

The past inhabitants of Zeeland through their journey of life have left the biggest proof of unity as a gift to all the citizens of this world. This unique story of unity proves when and where we stand together, we shall always be victorious. These unique and courageous inhabitants of Zeeland through their actions, from the Netherlands, shall be everblooming.

CHAPTER FOUR:

NOORD-BRABANT

"The skies above and the Earth beneath become one as the children upon Earth create a harmonious painting. The artists change, yet the Earth and the skies remain the same."

-Ann Marie Ruby

Noord-Brabant

NOORD-BRABANT

I welcomed historical figures,

As they had taken birth within my land.

You all know one of them as the great painter,

Vincent Willem van Gogh.

Within my city Eindhoven,

You shall greet the great statue of Philips,

One of my heroes.

My land welcomes your family and friends

To my great theme park Efteling.

Come and take a stroll through

My capital city, 's-Hertogenbosch.

Like all the other provinces

Within my country, the Netherlands,

I also have my own name,

As I am known

As the province

NOORD-BRABANT.

In the
southern part of
the Netherlands,
is North Brabant.
On her west, is Zeeland.
On her east, is Limburg.
To her north,
are South Holland
and Gelderland.

Welcome to Noord-Brabant (English: North Brabant). The capital of this province is 's-Hertogenbosch, which is also known as Den Bosch. This province had given birth to Hieronymus Bosch, who is known as one of the greatest painters of the early Renaissance period. In 1463, 's-Hertogenbosch had a catastrophic fire which had stayed within the minds of all whom witnessed it. Bosch who was thirteen years old at the time had seen this. A lot of people contribute one of Bosch's greatest creations ever, the fiery hellscape in *The Garden of Earthly Delights,* to this catastrophic fire.

One of the oldest amusement parks in the world, Efteling, began as a sports park in the 1930s in Kaatsheuvel, North Brabant. Since then, the park has evolved to become the great award-winning theme park that it is today. If only we could travel time and witness what the past inhabitants had lived like in those days. We can travel through the blessed pages of this book. Come time travel with me to the lives of the past.

THE HUMANITARIAN: FRITS PHILIPS

Eindhoven is the largest city in the province of North Brabant. Traveling to this city is easy as one can travel throughout the country without any worries. This city has the second largest airport of the Netherlands known as the Eindhoven Airport. Life is a blessing as we can travel from one part of this world to another with advanced technology.

Today, I want you to take a trip with me to the past during the time period of 1905 to 2005. Travel to the time period of a man who is known to have helped advance technology. He was the fourth chairman of the Dutch electronics company known to this world as Philips. Born into a very wealthy family, one would think he must be just another rich kid on the block. Yet, travel back in time and get to know him as a person admired yesterday, and who shall be admired throughout time.

World War II had changed the lives of all across this globe. The dark times had given us villains we all fear even to this day. Where did people go and hide when enemies were all around? How do your feet move when you freeze in fear? Would you be a person who saves oneself first and forgets the others?

Around the time the Nazis had entered the Netherlands in 1940, members of the Philips family had left to find refuge in the United States of America. Frederik Jacques "Frits" Philips, however, had stayed back during the catastrophic attacks. He could not go as he had to take care of not only his company but his employees.

During the period of May 30 to September 20, 1943, this great man was held at the Vught concentration camp because of a strike at his factory. Throughout the war, Philips put in a lot of effort to protect all his Jewish employees. He wanted to make sure they were getting meals. He made sure his Jewish employees received their salaries either during the war, or after they returned to work. Philips worked hard to prevent the deportation of his employees.

He insisted to the Nazis that his employees were needed to keep the Philips company running. For his insistence, his convincing skills, and his genuine care for his employees, Philips is said to have saved 382 of his Jewish employees. It takes a lot of courage to speak up in the time of war. In 1996, Philips was named as one of the Righteous Among the Nations by Yad Vashem.

Life is a journey through the lessons given to us by our past inhabitants. Some we are blessed to meet and some we meet through the pages of history. This is one such person I would have been blessed to have met, yet time separates us today. So, I am honored to be able to retell his blessed journey through history. I know blessed also were the people he was able to save.

Be an example by leading others to safety, not so by trying to be the leader. The examples left by an exemplary individual unite the past inhabitants with the present and the future. This unique individual selflessly chose to be an example for not just the past but all throughout time.

The chosen path of this individual has also gifted another chance of life for others who might not have had another chance in life. For this, he is an exemplary person who lived not only for himself but all of whom were blessed to meet him. For his actions, yesterday, today, and tomorrow, Frederik Jacques "Frits" Philips shall always be, from the Netherlands, everblooming.

COURAGEOUS DEED OF THE BRUININGS

North Brabant is a province where people had fought to keep their neighbors safe. Some had fought for their employees. What would we the present inhabitants do if someone we know is in danger? Would we only try to protect ourselves and our families? Or would humanity take over our fears? Let us go and travel time to see what a certain family had done, when they were placed in this situation.

During World War II, the predators were all over. The fearful night would bring them into the homes of all who were not like them, the Jews, Sinti, and Roma, resistance fighters, or anyone who disagreed with them. These dark enemies of the night are known to all as the Nazis. The howling huntsmen of World War II spread out all over the Netherlands, searching for their prey and all of whom gave shelter to their prey. A frightening night had brought these Nazis to the door of a family known as, the Bruinings.

Hajo Bruining was a physicist at the Philips Natuurkundig Laboratorium (English: Philips Physics Laboratory). He lived with his wife Nora and their four children. Through the war, Bruining was part of the Dutch resistance movement. He used a transmitter to speak with England. Even though he had young children, everyone knew to keep this a secret.

One chilling frightful night, there was a knock at the door. The uninvited guests, the Nazis, were at the door. They were looking for Bruining because somehow his resistance work fell under their radar. The whole family had to think quickly. On top of the Nazis looking for Bruining, he had helped hide a Jewish doctor named Betty Levi in their home. Bruining had risked his life and all of his family members' lives to do the humanly impossible job.

Quickly, Nora hid her husband under the floor. Their daughter Annette was sick and because of her illness, she had to be in bed. Nora moved Annette to her father's bed. When the Nazis entered the room, they saw the sickly child. Nora told them she had tuberculosis, and the Nazis being scared of the deadly disease did not want to touch the girl.

They quickly moved and continued to search the whole house. They found Levi in bed, but Nora was quick and talented as she told the Nazi hunters the woman was their nanny. The horrible night ended as the Nazis left satisfied with the story. All night, however, they stood guard outside. Bruining, with Nora's help, came out of hiding in the morning and found shelter in the Royal Psychiatric Hospital. If he were to stay at home, then he would put his family in danger because the Nazis were looking for him. He remained in hiding until Eindhoven was liberated.

The British government gave Bruining an award for his exceptional bravery and courage. They also made him a member of the Order of the British Empire. A wartime hero is not seen or remembered as only his deeds are remembered. Through his deeds, he teaches all of us throughout time. On that cold chilling night, Bruining was not looking for an award. He was only trying to save a life and keep his family safe. His family worked together, and all gave a helping hand. They became humanitarians before anything else. Awards are for us to remember him and his deeds.

Remember, his selfless deed to save an innocent woman will be our lesson throughout time. We should never forget his deed and his selfless act of humanity. The courageous Hajo Bruining and his family shall be within history from the Netherlands, forever everblooming.

THE MAN BEHIND THE CANVAS: VAN GOGH

"I dream of painting and then I paint my dream," said Vincent Willem van Gogh describing his passion of giving life to his dreams. He was a Post-Impressionist painter who loved his birthland, North Brabant. So many of his paintings tell a story of how he was inspired by his birthplace. He loved the night skies as he had said in many of his letters that he had sent to his brother, Theodorus "Theo" van Gogh.

"For my part I know nothing with any certainty, but the sight of the stars makes me dream." In this quote, Van Gogh talks about his love for nature which he portrayed throughout his life on Earth. He was born on March 30, 1853 in Zundert, the Netherlands. He died in Auvers-sur-Oise, France on July 29, 1890. Let us travel through time and get to know an artist who had captured so much love within his paintings.

Van Gogh's love for his land and people found its way within his artwork created with his own hands. North Brabant, his childhood land, had created the painter in him. If you walk to his birthplace, now the famous museum, the Vincent van GoghHuis (English: Vincent van Gogh House) in Zundert, you too can see his love for his land. Even though in 1903, the original home where the famous painter was born had been demolished, today there is a plaque on the wall where he was born.

Van Gogh is known to have collected people from the real world as his subjects for his work. He wanted people to be real, not dressed up in their best attires. The painter loved to recreate the village cottages as his eyes saw them. The famous artist found so much love in his work, but never found romantic love in his personal life. Stories are said about his search for love which left him wondering about the woman who would love him like he loved his art. Life is not always fair as he had fallen for a few women, but these were one-sided love stories as his dream girl never appeared.

After several rejections, Van Gogh had helped a pregnant prostitute in The Hague in 1882. He fell in love with the prostitute and they lived together for a while, but his family never accepted the prostitute named, Clasina Maria "Sien" Hoornik. This relationship also came to an end as things did not work out. Van Gogh had said, "For my part, I still continually have the most impossible and highly unsuitable love affairs from which, as a rule, I emerge only with shame and disgrace."

After more failed attempts at love, he began to paint in theaters and dance halls in Antwerp, Belgium in 1885. Prostitutes were often the subject of his paintings. After this period, he had moved to Paris, where he had not only painted the city life but also brothels. It was then he had more failed love attempts. Van Gogh had tried to ask for help as he had continued to write letters to his brother Theo. Theo loved his brother and tried to help him. Yet after years of mental illness, a failed love life, and failed commercial success, Van Gogh fell into grave depression.

Van Gogh had admitted himself into a mental asylum for one year, where he felt better and painted many of his now incredibly famous works of art, such as *The Starry Night*. After leaving the asylum, the great painter eventually succumbed to injuries two days after a gunshot to his chest, at the age of only thirty-seven. Maybe Van Gogh was describing his life as he said, "I put my heart and my soul into my work, and have lost my mind in the process."

Van Gogh's paintings are found all throughout this world. Today, we have over 2,100 artworks of this famous painter. When he was alive, however, neither did his paintings nor his knocking on doors for help reach the ears of those who could help. After this great painter was lost, even to this day, there are rumors surrounding his death. People are trying to figure out was it self-inflicted or was it murder? Historically, it has been accepted that Van Gogh had committed suicide.

He had given us enormous gifts, but it seems as though we as a society were not able to help him. He asked, sought, and knocked for help. Somehow, his cries did not reach the ears of those who could help.

It seems like sometimes, a simple acknowledgement of love prevails the pain. Ultimately, rejection in love life, financial hurdles, or always being criticized by a family whose traditional lifestyles might not match yours could be a trigger for the worse.

Accept the differences within society, family, and friends. Not everyone's desired ways of life are the same or to another's acceptance. Is life to please the other or please oneself? This is a question I ask as I walk through the past lives. I believe we all have the right to live our own way to our heart's desires but including our loved ones somehow.

Maybe it would help if our loved ones meet us in the middle and include themselves as love is a two-way bridge. One person cannot hold on to both sides and make the bridge stable. Life is short and I personally believe life is a day. It begins at dawn and ends at dusk, so we must live this day completely like there is no other day.

The travelers who today are traveling upon the same path where the great artist Van Gogh had walked, I hope you will keep asking, seeking, and knocking for help. Do not stop searching for the helping hand, for there is always a helping hand. Where there is hope, there is a way. This is a message from the past that guides us not to stop seeking for help.

This amazing painter throughout his life lived had framed within his canvas, artwork that shall talk throughout time. Sometimes, even though the person is no more, a poet leaves behind his poetry, a singer his song, and an artist his art which communicates from the past to the future. Vincent Willem van Gogh through his artwork and his life has communicated with all the inhabitants of this world, from the Netherlands, as he was and shall always be everblooming.

CHAPTER FIVE:

UTRECHT

"Be happy and spread happiness from today, tomorrow, and yesterdays. As this message reaches you, do remember to inscribe these beautiful memories of happiness within your inner soul."

-Ann Marie Ruby

Utrecht

UTRECHT

This world is one home

As we are all blessed happily ever after.

Be happy and live happily is the lesson,

You will learn as you enter my land.

I can be seen from far and near

As I have the highest church tower within my country.

My Domtoren too greets you as it is blessed

With tourist friends from my country and the one world.

My land is the birthplace of our great and honorable King,

His Majesty, King Willem-Alexander.

The King's mother, the beloved former Queen,

Her Royal Highness, Princess Beatrix lives here.

When visiting me, do stroll by

And get to know my capital city Utrecht.

I am the smallest province in the Netherlands.

Just like my capital city, I too am known

As the province

UTRECHT.

In the middle of
the Netherlands,
is Utrecht.
On her west and southwest,
is South Holland.
On her east and southeast, is
Gelderland.
To her north and northwest,
is North Holland.
To her north and northeast,
is Flevoland.

Welcome to Utrecht. The capital of this province is the city of Utrecht. His Majesty, King Willem-Alexander was born in Utrecht. His mother, the former Queen, Her Royal Highness Princess Beatrix again made Utrecht her home after her abdication. This province is also home to the UNESCO World Heritage Site, the Rietveld Schröderhuis (English: Rietveld Schröder House). This house is famous for its use of De Stijl and modern architecture by the architect Gerrit Thomas Rietveld.

For centuries, Utrecht has been the religious center. The tallest church tower of the Netherlands, the famous Domtoren (English: Dom Tower) is in this province. The only Dutch pope, Pope Adrian VI, was from Utrecht.

Come with me and let us go back in time to get acquainted with a few faces from the past.

JUSTICE FOUND AT OUDEWATER

A star-filled night had guided me to a small town within the province of Utrecht, known as Oudewater. This place had a welcoming feeling. I had to walk back in time to get in touch with the previous visitors. The wagon of time had kept us apart but from the pages of memories, I united with them. Come travel with me as you too can get yourself acquainted with another part of our unjust history. This history, however, had shown hope for the visitors of the past.

During the medieval period, weighing scales were common. People would weigh their crops and livestock. Slowly, people started to weigh humans too. These humans were accused of being witches. Anyone out of anger, for revenge, or out of fear for no reason, could bring in a charge against any person of being a witch. To prove a person was a witch was easy, yet to prove someone was not a witch was extremely hard as the whole system was rigged.

A neighbor could accuse another person of practicing witchcraft on his crops. A neighbor would bring a sickly child and say a certain person has bewitched her. If a person could heal another person with the help of herbs, she would be accused of being a witch, after the healing process had taken place. Another way in which witches were accused was by tying them and letting them float in the water. If they floated, then they were accused of being a witch. If they drowned, then they just died and would be pronounced not a witch. All over Europe, the burning of witches had begun.

People tried to get justice from far and near. Humans were weighed at weighing houses to see if one would weigh anything. The belief was witches cannot have any weight because otherwise they would not float or fly. In 1545, the Holy Roman Emperor, Charles V, was unsure about the outcome of a woman's weight. He had asked a woman to be reweighed at Oudewater. The woman was weighed and was found to weigh around 100 pounds (45 kilograms). The woman was saved from being burned at the stake. Horrible punishments were laid out for people who were found guilty.

In Oudewater, no one was found guilty. The people there refused to take bribes and commit any sins. All the people who were able to get themselves to Oudewater, were set free. The people working there refused to rig the blessed weighing scale. The Holy Roman Emperor, Charles V, recognized this weighing house as being fair. All who passed the weighing test received a special certificate. The blessed weighhouse in Oudewater is known as Museum de Heksenwaag (English: Witches' Weighhouse Museum).

You can come here and have your weight taken. Get a certificate for fun to clear any accusation of you being a witch. Remember, so many accused witches only dreamed of being able to go there and get their names cleared. Today, you can give your neighbors a recipe for treating a cold and not worry about the same neighbor accusing you of being a witch. I wonder how many of you have ever gone to a psychic or looked up your own horoscope on the internet, yet you will not be accused of being a witch.

History teaches us and shows us how our own superstitious minds can be dangerous for oneself and others. If you would like to give another person anything, then give your forgiveness and blessings. Do not take the law in your own hands and do not be the judge, for history with her wagon shall judge you.

Innocence found her voice shouting louder than above the sky in Heaven. Yet innocence down on Earth found no shelter until the accused were able to come to this blessed house where a human could be weighed to prove his or her innocence. This proves even when injustice is done, somewhere on Earth, justice prevails. Not a person, not a group, but here a house talks for her inhabitants to whom she was able to bring justice. Here, the Heksenwaag of Oudewater will be remembered throughout time from the Netherlands as everblooming.

KNIGHT OF
KASTEEL DE HAAR

The sky was pouring. I felt she was cleaning all the pain from this world on the day I had traveled to the province of Utrecht. A beautiful park-like setting welcomes you as you enter the magnificent castle called Kasteel de Haar (English: De Haar Castle). De Haar Castle is the largest castle in the Netherlands. This famous castle is in the village of Haarzuilens.

The castle was owned by the Van de Haar family in 1391. The final heir died without any male heir in 1440. So, the castle changed owners and the new owner was the Van Zuylen family. Baron Etienne van Zuylen van Nijevelt van de Haar, had inherited this castle in 1890. He was married to Hélène de Rothschild, a very wealthy bride who had restored this building as a wedding gift. The renovation had lasted twenty years. The property remained within the family and now the castle is property of the Kasteel de Haar Foundation.

As you visit, do see the interior of the knight's hall. It has hooks on the ceiling to catch ghosts as described by the tour guides. If you visit other medieval buildings, you might see hooks on the ceiling. It was believed the hooks would capture ghosts which would disappear when the sun came out at dawn.

Maybe the following legend would give some clues as to why De Haar Castle is rumored to be haunted. The legend that has been passed on orally is that a knight is frequently seen strolling in the castle. The fifteenth century legend goes as follows.

A very arrogant and ignorant knight had lived in the castle. Once a beggar woman had asked for food and shelter for a night. The knight was very arrogant and wanted to scare her off with his horse. The knight was fully armored in his knightly attire. He was so heavy, he could not maneuver himself. It is said, the knight and his horse both slipped, fell into the moat, and drowned. The knight was never seen alive again, yet his ghost still roams the castle.

Maybe this is by chance, but the castle does have a tower with a statue of a knight standing tall. I do not know about the ghosts of the past, but all people living or dead must find their peace through forgiveness. Life is a journey through blessings and struggles. Arrogance and ignorance are not virtues. We, the humans, must not carry these sinful burdens upon our shoulders. Throughout this journey of life, we forget we the humans are all temporary guests upon this Earth.

Watch out for all whom you cross through this journey of life. If you cannot give them your helping hands, do try not to step over them. The wagon of karma follows you throughout this life and even in the beyond.

The story of the knight might be a legend or a true story, but the castle is not a legend as it still exists. When you visit the castle, do appreciate the restoration it underwent and all the past inhabitants who had left behind their stories which we might never know or yet might know. What we do know is this amazing castle holds within itself a gift for all of its visitors.

How people had lived there and where they had cooked, the knights and the guards, all of them had a story to tell. This castle today is open to all visitors without any discrimination. So, I believe the castle is in itself reminding everyone you might discriminate against race, color, religion, high class, or low class of the society, but this castle does not as all people across the globe enter this amazing castle. De Haar Castle is letting the world know as it was here in the past, it is here in the present, and it shall always be here in the future accepting visitors from around the globe as the largest castle from the Netherlands remains everblooming.

TEACHER'S UMBRELLA: CAECILIA LOOTS

A teacher's journey continues throughout time. As a child, I thought my teacher could fix anything. I believed teachers could heal wounds, wipe tears, teach math, and maybe if asked, they could bring the stars down to us. My father had always told me, the stars upon the skies were his best friends. I had as a child told him, I would ask my teacher to bring the stars down upon Earth as a gift to him. Today, I know my father has left and taken his place in the skies with his best friends.

I want all of you to hold my hands as we now journey back to 1942. It was then a teacher had done the unexpected task and kept her children safe. She prevented the children from becoming a night star upon the skies. She wanted these children to shine like the biggest star, the sun, during their time on Earth and have a complete life.

During World War II, we find people with humanity walking for one another. Their thought was not about self-protection but all others who need safety and needed to be protected. Caecilia Antonia Maria "Cilia" Loots, a devout

Catholic teacher for children with severe learning disabilities, was asked to take in some Jewish children.

Without even thinking twice, she took in all the children who came upon her door. She kept the children hidden within her home and kept their lessons going on. She hid the children in her attic. Even though her own life was at risk, this did not prevent a human from doing the right thing.

Loots kept all the children safe within her home which was located within the vicinity of a German camp. Throughout this time, she had a helping hand, by the name of Dina van Heiningen. Van Heiningen knew about the whole situation and without letting fear win, she helped keep all of the children safe and the situation a secret. She helped with all the housework as the number of children had increased slowly. They also gave shelter to adults.

Religious differences are only within the eyes of the divider. Within the soul of a teacher, Loots only saw her children, not a religious group. Teachers call their students, their own children. A mother keeps her children safe from the cold by wrapping her child within a shawl. Here, a teacher had kept the children safe within her home, protecting them from the enemy. The children loved Loots and called her Tante Ciel (English: Aunt Ciel). She was recognized in 1969 and named Righteous Among the Nations by Yad Vashem.

Today in 2020, as we live in a very divided world, I would ask all of you to take a trip down the memory lane with Loots. A teacher still teaches from the past. Her lessons have not ended as long as we the present keep sharing her taught lessons. From the diaries of the past, I want all of you to carry this page along within your neighborhoods.

Share this message with everyone today to learn and teach the future generations that there is only one race, one color, one religion, known as we, the humans. Loots, a teacher, even after death unites all through her left lessons. As we relive through the journey of her life, we learn another lesson of humanity. Throughout time, Caecilia Antonia Maria "Cilia" Loots will be remembered as a teacher who never stopped teaching as her story shall always be from the Netherlands, everblooming.

CHAPTER SIX:

FLEVOLAND

"Lessons of life are found within a teacher's journal for it is the student's survival guide on how to build, not give up."

-Ann Marie Ruby

FLEVOLAND

Come sit with my inhabitants and

Meet the old and new fishermen of the past and present.

Here you can listen to the stories of Urk and the Urkers,

And how Schokland was an island

Before it became a ghost town.

Lelystad is my capital city.

When you stand upon my chest,

Do remember I was a part of the Zuiderzee.

I have been reclaimed

From the sea by the children of my land.

I have the largest reclaimed

Human-made island in the world, the Flevopolder,

And this is my birth story.

Do come and witness the miracle of my existence

As you walk upon my chest.

I am the youngest province as I am the twelfth province.

Within my country, the Netherlands, you all know me

As the province

FLEVOLAND.

In the middle of
the Netherlands,
is Flevoland.
The Markermeer and IJsselmeer
lakes hug her on the northwest.
On her northeast, is Overijssel.
To her southwest, are Utrecht
and North Holland.
To her southeast,
is Gelderland.
To her north,
is Friesland.

Welcome to Flevoland. The capital of this province is Lelystad. Flevoland was established January 1, 1986 making it the twelfth and youngest province in the Netherlands. This province is an example for the world as the largest land reclamation project. Most of the residents in this province now live on land that used to be the seafloor of the Zuiderzee (English: Southern Sea).

In this province, you, the world citizen, can take a lesson in how the Dutch reclaimed their land. Today, they go around the globe teaching other low-lying countries how to save their lands. Flevoland is also called the world's largest shipwreck graveyard as it is reported within this province, more than 450 wrecks were discovered.

What once was the seafloor, now actually has the largest flower fields. There is a scenic tulip route, around 50 miles (80 kilometers) long, which you can drive through. Now, let us take a journey and pay a visit to some inhabitants of the past from the province of Flevoland.

LIGHTHOUSE KEEPER OF SCHOKLAND: JACOB VAN EERDE

A lighthouse glows even through the dark starless nights. Like a candle of hope, she glows yet there must be someone who keeps the lighthouse lighted with his or her blessed hands. A mother watching over her children keeps the burning candles glowing. Even though she burns her hands, she protects the candles to keep them glowing through the dark stormy nights. In Schokland, the blessed lighthouse keeper would keep the lighthouse glowing through the wild storms of the sea.

Let us travel time to the 1800s. In 1859, by the order of King William III, most of the island had been evacuated. The reasoning was an ongoing battle with the ravishing floods and storms. On March 1, 1859, the then mayor Gerrit Jan Gillot announced all residents to leave, excluding the lighthouse keeper and essential government employees. The lighthouse keeper's job was essential as the lighthouse was not yet automated.

In the early 1900s, Jacob van Eerde was the lighthouse keeper and his brother Teunis helped him in

Schokland. The lighthouse keeper and his brother were basically left alone on Schokland with some essential government employees. So, the lighthouse keeper and his brother lived on an island but did not have much interaction with other humans as the island was basically empty.

Life became very lonely and depressing. Even essential employees slowly left or had passed away. Slowly, the sea brought skeletons of dead bodies out of an old graveyard, making it even more disturbing for the brothers. The brothers slowly started to get cabin fever. Their situation deteriorated to a point where they were mentally unstable because of their loneliness and isolation.

Eventually in 1911, they had to leave because of their mental deterioration. The lighthouse keeper eventually did recover. His brother also lived, but it is said only the lighthouse keeper had married and had children. Now, as I write this book in 2020, we the world citizens face one of the biggest catastrophic pandemics of recent times. We, the present-day citizens, know how it feels to be lonely as so many are asked to be quarantined. The seclusion is hard as one cannot go anywhere. Even when you feel like you cannot stay inside anymore, you must.

Despite the pandemic, essential employees continue to provide their services. I know and have witnessed how the medical providers are taking on this mental toll. The lives for which they have taken an oath to save, they now watch die in mass numbers in front of them.

We must take a step back and realize how loneliness and mental stress can impact the human mind, body, and soul. The lighthouse keepers stay within the tower to guide all safely through the waters. We must be there for them and let them know we the world citizens too care for them.

Remember this lighthouse and its keepers who at the cost of their own selves had shown the past the way back home. When you visit the UNESCO World Heritage Site, Schokland, you too can be the candle of hope today by keeping their memories alive. I only wonder how many ships were guided back to safety with the hands of the lighthouse keeper. Within the books of history, Jacob van Eerde has made himself a space where he shall be from the Netherlands, everblooming.

VISIONS OF
HENDRIC STEVIN AND
CORNELIS LELY

The inner eyes see the concepts and eventually they find life through the plans conceived. Here, a dreamer had envisioned a dream and this dream had waited out its time to become reality. This dreamer was Hendric Stevin and his dream would make Flevoland the largest land reclamation project in the world.

Come with me as we travel time to see the mind of a dreamer who had through the blessed hands of time and technology converted his dream into reality. Not only did this genius mind prove he can conceive this, he also proved one lifetime is enough if you can only get the inspiration going. Through the wagon of inspiration, the future generations do complete the projects you had begun. Without ever moving from your own place, you have just asked another person to get you the cold glass of water your heart so desired.

Stevin, a hydraulic engineer, knew water had dominated their lives. He wanted to befriend water, not be scared of it. His thought was, what if we could tame the untamable water? In 1667, he published an innovative plan for the Netherlands in the twelfth volume of his *Wisconstich Filosofisch Bedrijf*. The Zuiderzee which was an inlet body of water off the North Sea would often flood the surrounding land. Stevin had written a plan that would allow the Dutch to have more control over the Zuiderzee to stop these recurring floods.

In Stevin's plan, a system of dikes would be built from North Holland up north to block off the Zuiderzee from the North Sea. He also planned to drain water out of the Zuiderzee. Stevin had a good idea to prevent future flooding and reclaim land. His way of thinking, however, was ahead of his time as technology had not advanced enough to be capable of executing his plan. Even then, he kept his concept alive through his faith in the concept.

After Stevin, others tried to develop plans based on his idea. It was not until Cornelis Lely created his plan in the late 1800s, that action was taken. By then, technology and engineering were both more advanced than they were during Stevin's time period. So, here through the wagon of time, Lely and Stevin were invisibly tied through their wish to tame the untamable sea.

The Zuiderzee Act was passed on June 14, 1918 clearing the way for the project Zuiderzee Works. Over the next few years, the construction work began. The Dutch have a saying that "God created the Earth, but the Dutch created the Netherlands." This reclamation project proves how even throughout time, humans worked in union to reclaim land they all call home.

Neither Stevin nor Lely were able to see their plans completely fulfilled. Yet, through the wagon of time, over three hundred years after Stevin's time period, we now have the newest province of Flevoland established in 1986. Flevoland is a province created mostly from islands and land that was reclaimed from the Zuiderzee.

The Dutch indeed were able to take control of the Zuiderzee and prevent flooding. The whole engineering project of the Zuiderzee Works along with the Delta Works is known as one of the Seven Wonders of the Modern World. Now when you walk upon this project or even drive through this wonder, do accept the gifts of the past geniuses by remembering them.

Even though time passes by us, as we are always left behind in the past, remember your thoughts or dreams will be picked up by another in the future. True, you might not know this person but he or she knows you through admiration of you, your thoughts, and your dreams. The bond through time is made through admiration, the admirers, and the admired.

I believe, dreams are just that, dreams, until we convert them into reality. Stevin and Lely have through time converted their dreams into reality. Stevin's vision required other visionaries from the future to guide the past, present, and future into safety. A bridge was created through time.

This dream that a person in the past had was completed through his determination. Life might come to an end, yet true visions will be passed on to the hands of future visionaries who will complete the job. This fate has made Hendric Stevin and Cornelis Lely, from the Netherlands, everblooming.

AN ARTIST OF URK: JAN VISSCHER

Welcome to Urk, a municipality in the province of Flevoland. Urk was once an island, but on October 3, 1939, as a part of the Zuiderzee Works, a dike was made to connect Urk to Lemmer, a town in Friesland. As land was reclaimed around Urk, the former island Urk became part of the mainland. Even though it is no longer an island, Urk is home to one of the largest fishing fleets in the Netherlands, and one of the largest fish markets in Europe.

Come travel time with me to an old fishermen's village where the fishermen, their wives, and their children had lived on an island years ago. Let us go to a time of simplicity, not in the movies or a portrait, but in the past to a time when life was a wishing tree of dreams. The lighthouse that guides all even on this day is the same lighthouse which had guided all in the past.

If only the lighthouse could speak and tell us all the stories of the past. We could all sit in the harbor and listen to the memories of the lighthouse. The bridge of memories would guide today's fishermen through the learned lessons of the past fishermen. Through the door of memories, let me take you to the yesteryears of Urk.

Within this island, lived a fisherman who was also an artist by the name of Jan Visscher. Visscher was born in 1855 and passed away in 1938, before Urk became part of the mainland. He loved the sea and all of the sea's surroundings. Visscher performed all of his work by the sea.

He enjoyed sitting on the deck by the sea with his kitchen scissors. Using this big pair of scissors, he clipped papers and created art from them. This is why he is also known as Jan de Knipper or Jantje de Knipper (English: Jan the Clipper).

He made scenes from the Bible and his fisherman life including the church and lighthouse. Sometimes with cut-out letters, he would create Biblical scenes from the Genesis such as Adam and Eve. As a fisherman, Visscher had time to do this artwork. It is said he may have been illiterate as he would mix up uppercase and lowercase letters. Even though he may have been illiterate, his work was amazing.

When he worked in the harbor, he would have interactions with visitors who had come to the island of Urk. Visscher would sell his artwork to these visitors. He did not expect fame, and the buying costs were only a few cents each as he loved to create them more than the profit.

His artwork did not have the value or appreciation during his time, but now a collection of his artwork sits proudly at the Museum Het Oude Raadhuis (English: The Old Townhall Museum) of Urk. Visscher is now an artist whose work is visited by people from around the world. Numerous works of his art were donated by visitors whose relatives had bought them from the fisherman in the past.

Life is a journey through time where we must complete our journeys to become complete. Some are relatively successful during their travel on this Earth. Some on the other hand, are only recognized after their journey has ended upon Earth. We the humans must not stop living at our success or failure as the journey is not yet complete. Life and its journey are a travel guide for the future travelers.

We the travelers now have the story of an artist who once had been on the island of Urk creating his artwork. Through his art collection, we shall always be connected to this great artist of the past and his amazing fishermen's village, Urk. Today, tomorrow, or in the near future, when a traveler happens to stop by at Museum Het Oude Raadhuis, remember this great artist was once here creating his art. All he needed was paper and a pair of scissors. Through his work left behind for we the world citizens, Jan Visscher shall be remembered from the Netherlands as everblooming.

CHAPTER SEVEN:

FRIESLAND

"Languages create a great bond between friends, as you keep your own and accept the others into one home of the one family."

-Ann Marie Ruby

Friesland

FRIESLAND

My green agricultural land is pleasing

To all of my inhabitants and visitors,

As I am a pleasure to the eyes.

The Wadden Islands in the Wadden Sea

Welcome all peace-loving and harmonious visitors

With memorable memories.

My inhabitants have their own language,

West Frisian in addition to Dutch.

Here we have created our largest steam pumping station,

The Ir. D.F. Woudagemaal.

My land welcomes you to her.

Stop by our capital city Leeuwarden

As you come and visit.

For all of you,

I am known within my country, the Netherlands,

As the province

FRIESLAND.

In the northern part
of the Netherlands,
is Friesland.
The Wadden Sea hugs her
on the north.
On her east, is Groningen.
On her southwest,
is North Holland.
On her southeast, are Drenthe
and Overijssel.
To her south, is Flevoland.

Welcome to Friesland (West Frisian: Fryslân). The capital of this province is Leeuwarden. Friesland is part of the historical region known as Frisia. Aside from Dutch, the native tongue here is West Frisian. The Wadden Sea on the coast of Friesland is a nature reserve, listed as a UNESCO World Heritage Site since 2009. The largest steam pumping station, Ir. D.F. Woudagemaal, has also been listed by UNESCO as a World Heritage Site since 1998.

This province is commonly referred to as one of the hidden gems in Europe. Truly a beautiful province, tourists should spend some time here before leaving this country. As you get acquainted with the present-day Friesland, let us go back in time and get acquainted with some of the past residents.

EISE EISINGA'S DETERMINATION

Eighteenth-century inhabitants of the city of Franeker in Friesland meet us through the pages of history. Let us travel to a time when fear had gripped the citizens after a Dutch preacher had made his prediction. What do we do when a prediction is made but the answer is written only in the wagon of the future?

The prediction in question was made by a Dutch preacher named Eelco Alta in April 1774. His prediction was the world would end soon because of the alignment of the planets. His thought was the planets Mercury, Venus, Mars, and Jupiter as well the moon and their positioning on May 8, 1774 would cause a catastrophe. According to Alta, the positioning of the planets would cause Earth to be pushed off its track and be burned by the sun. This prediction had people go into turmoil as all fell into fear.

One person did not accept this theory. Instead of having the town break out in panic, he wanted to relieve them from this stress. Let us make a trip to this particular time period and be the guest of a certain person who had taken upon his hands a big challenge.

Meet Eise Jeltes Eisinga, a professional wool comber, who loved mathematics and astronomy so much that he tutored himself on these subjects. He did not believe in the preacher's prediction and started to prove his theory as he began building the solar system on his living room ceiling. He wanted all to see for themselves what the solar system actually looked like and how it functioned. It, however, had taken him seven years to finish as his project was finally complete in 1781.

Eisinga's planetarium has all the mechanical movements of the sun, Mercury, Venus, Earth, Mars, Jupiter, Saturn, and all the moons associated with each of the planets. The discovery of Uranus was made in the same year, but there was no more space on his living room ceiling. Neptune was not discovered until much later in 1846.

The planetarium was so accurate, one would not even know or believe this was the creation of someone who was not an astronomer or a mathematician. This was the creation of a person who loved what he did. It started as a challenge and an answer to the questions of the questioners who thought the world was going to end. King William I was so amazed by the planetarium after his visit in 1818, that he had bought the planetarium for the Dutch State.

Today, you too can visit this amazing site which was nominated in 2011 to be a UNESCO World Heritage Site. This is the oldest planetarium on Earth that is still functioning. When visiting, do not criticize the preacher who only tried to help and made a wrong prediction. Yet, do honor the determination and brilliance of a great man who had stood alone and showed he was right.

Believe in yourself even though you might stand alone. Alone on a lonely road you might be, not believed by anyone but yourself. It is better to stand alone on the right path rather than in a crowd on the wrong path. Time passes by as lessons are learned only through the journey of the traveler who has crossed time.

This traveler believed in himself and worked to prove himself. Today, when you visit the Royal Eise Eisinga Planetarium, do remember through his hands, patience, and belief, he left behind an amazing creation. This invention of a determined citizen has placed himself in the pages of history where this world will always find him, Eise Jeltes Eisinga from the Netherlands, everblooming.

FRISIAN MIDWIFE: CATHARINA SCHRADER

Friesland, a province in the Netherlands, may feel like a different country as many speak in West Frisian. Framed by the Wadden Sea, Friesland is a beautiful piece of paradise that meets the eyes as you greet her at dawn. The glorious sunsets are enriched by the life stories of the past inhabitants.

One such inhabitant was a kindhearted soul who was very stern, yet the past, the present, and I know the future too shall admire her. Let us travel to the year 1656 when a child was born in Germany by the name of Catharina Geertruida Schrader. Schrader eventually ended up in Friesland, the Netherlands, where she spent the rest of her days, famously known as the Frisian Midwife and a diarist.

Love finds all as we search for it. Schrader too found her first love and married Ernst Wilhelm Cramer, a surgeon, in 1683, with whom she had a total of six children. They had settled in Hallum, Friesland. Life does play its own way as in 1692, Schrader was left a widow with the death of her husband. With six children to raise, she soon began to work as a midwife. She had some experience helping her husband in delivering babies, and she had read textbooks about midwifery.

When and where one has nothing, it is then we know from heavens above someone must be guiding. Schrader was devoted to her religion and believed her faith had called upon her. She believed it was the Lord's calling for her to become a midwife. In 1695, Schrader, had taken all her children and moved to Dokkum to reduce her commute to work.

As a midwife, she helped deliver over three thousand babies, and had over 90% successful births. At the beginning, however, she had asked others to help her. As she became more and more experienced, others contacted her for help, especially for riskier situations.

From 1693 to 1745, Schrader wrote down details of the deliveries she had helped with in a diary. The purpose of this diary was to help future midwives. She wanted others to learn from her experiences, her mistakes, and what she had done in risky cases. This diary would be her gift for the future.

Schrader even took note of her accounting. As a midwife, she was earning a good income. She was earning two hundred to three hundred guilders per year. She was well respected and did not look at any group of people different from another. She helped the rich and the poor. Her fee was not fixed as it was different based on who she was helping and how much they could pay. Sometimes, she was not paid and she had a list of these people in her diary.

In 1713, Schrader married the mayor of Dokkum, Thomas Higt. As her fate would have it, he too would pass away within a decade and she would become a widow again. During her marriage, she worked less and helped deliver her own grandchildren. When her husband passed away, she no longer had to work for money. Yet, Schrader believed it was her calling to help other people, so she continued once again as a midwife into her old age when she was eighty-eight years old.

The personal diary Schrader had kept to guide future generations was made into a book, *Memoryboeck van de Vrouwens* (English: Memory Book of the Women). Schrader always started the new year with a prayer written in her diary. As you walk through her book, do know even today many Dutch women still favor home delivery.

Wherever you choose to give birth, people like Schrader are still out there. This person may be your gynocologist, midwife, or even a friend. They are there to guide another person into this world. Through this new life, you are connected to the future. Women like Schrader are always connected to the present and future through all the lives brought into this world.

The birth of a child is one of the best yet at the same time, one of the most riskiest parts of being a woman. During this time, all women need a helping hand. Schrader had helped give birth not only to her time period, but future generations who will continue to blossom because their parents survived birth.

A complete miracle takes a complete circle through life. Schrader has traveled time through the children she helped give birth to and their future. As always, Catharina Geertruida Schrader, a giver of life, will be remembered from the Netherlands as everblooming.

A FRISIAN DAUGHTER: SASKIA VAN UYLENBURGH

Time and tide fly by, as we are left with memories of the bygone eras. Some memories gift us with famous names. This story, however, frames a face of the Dutch Golden Age who is not well known to all through her life lived. The love of her life, however, is well known, and it is through his eyes we find her.

Through the eyes of a lover, we find the eyes of a beloved. In this story, let us meet a woman who found her place in history through the eyes of the famous painter, Rembrandt Harmenszoon van Rijn. The spotlight of this story is not on the famous painter but his beloved wife, who had inspired him to give her eternal life within his portraits.

Saskia van Uylenburgh found the love of her life, one of the greatest painters of all time, when she visited her cousin Hendrick van Uylenburgh. Saskia grew up in Leeuwarden in a well-off family. She, however, fell in love with the painter who also fell deeply in love with her. Their love story had a nice beginning as they got married in 1634. Life is a journey where at times we get only one day and at times we get many years. This loving couple had ten beautiful and sad years together.

During their marriage, Saskia gave birth to four children of which one son survived into adulthood. Saskia had likely succumbed to tuberculosis at age twenty-nine in 1642. She was an incredibly lucky person to be so gravely loved by her husband. She was the artist's inspiration on his canvas and had been the model for many of his portraits. She left this world, but never did she leave his eyes. The painter loved to paint his wife and through his work, he left behind his signature proof of their love story.

Their love story had ended at Saskia's death. He stopped oil paintings for many years and his painting style had changed. Later periods showed grief and sadness. The famous painter had another chapter added to his life as he did have other relationships. None of these relationships would be like the one he had with Saskia. Their son died in 1668, a year before Rembrandt passed away.

This story, however, only talks about a wife who had loved her husband so much that she devoted her complete life to him. She had helped him even after her death as he was financially ruined and had no option but to sell her grave for financial needs. This is a sad love story where the musical notes of pain and sadness fill the air. How much did the daughter of Friesland, Saskia, love her husband that she even helped him from beneath her grave?

She had moved to Amsterdam with her husband to have a complete life full of memories. Her life was short with a bag full of sorrows, but she was loved by her husband. The sorrows they shared, the love they shared for one another, and she proved she still loved him after death as she helped him even then. Love is eternal even when life is not. A famous painter leaves behind his paintings for the world but keeps within his soul the eternal love for her through all his mistakes and achievements. Life is a day or a hundred years, it matters not, for love is eternal throughout time.

Everything in life fades away as do time and tide. Nevertheless, the high tides left behind by the past travelers reach our feet as we stand on the same shore. Touch the waves and feel their love, joy, and tears, as you too leave behind your love, joy, and tears. Through this path, we the past and present are tied in a bond even with our future.

Saskia was tied in a bond with her husband Rembrandt. Remember the famous phrase, "Behind every successful man, there stands a woman" as this phrase takes a life in this story. A beloved wife with her love had become a painter's life. She had given him the inspiration to paint from behind. Today, from the future, we forever shall know behind this great painter was a great wife, Saskia van Uylenburgh, who shall always be remembered from the Netherlands as everblooming.

CHAPTER EIGHT:

GRONINGEN

"Awaken within the picturesque canvas your immortal love. Rejuvenate within the beautiful landscape and know true love is found here as you spread your beauty from soul to soul throughout time."

-Ann Marie Ruby

Groningen

GRONINGEN

I welcome all of my inhabitants

To my large agricultural land.

You have entered my land to learn more about this Earth

As have so many students from around the globe.

Come and learn from the students of today

And the teachers of tomorrow as you visit my land.

My Martinitoren finds visitors enter her.

As they take back memories,

They leave behind some memories too.

The Wadden Sea welcomes you

Within the fresh rejuvenated air.

As you stand by the shore,

You will feel your rejuvenated soul.

Gather up in my capital city,

Known as the city of Groningen.

Let us greet and meet,

As I am known

As the province

GRONINGEN.

In the
most northeastern part of
the Netherlands,
is Groningen.
The Wadden Sea hugs her
on the north.
On her west,
is Friesland.
To her south,
is Drenthe.

Welcome to Groningen. The capital of this province is the city of Groningen. The city of Groningen has a diverse student population. It is called a very vibrant city for this reason. This city's pubs are kept open far later than any other city in the Netherlands. Groningen is also home to the famous Martinitoren (English: St. Martin's Tower).

This province borders the Wadden Sea which is a UNESCO World Heritage Site. An interesting site within this province is the Vesting Bourtange (English: Fort Bourtange). The beautiful fort was built in the shape of a star in 1593. Tourists can visit this fort today and appreciate the Dutch ingenuity in building this centuries ago.

Now let us go back in time to the years of the past inhabitants of Groningen. Come with me and let us together pay them a visit.

UNJUST JUSTICE OF WESTERWOLDE: ALKE ENGELS

In Westerwolde, there is a hill where green grass grows. Small trees cover the amazing picturesque landscape. Yet, this art is within the eyes of the beholders for within some eyes, this picture contains horrific screams, heart-gripping cries, and painful pleas that went unheard by the unjust justice of the powerful greed of man.

Come travel with me to the time period from 1587 to 1597, a very unjust period of humanity. During this time, a simple argument, jealousy, revenge, or just greed could get the powerful voices their unjust win. On this hill known as the Geselberg (English: Torture Hill), witches were burned at the stake.

The executions and burning of twenty-two people were reported within a decade. The accused would be subject to a water test in which they would be tied and thrown into the water. If they floated, they would be considered a witch. Then, they would be tortured and burned at the stake on the hill. The trial used to be held at the Burcht Wedde (English: Castle Wedde).

A pastor of Blijham by the name of Ludolphus Antonius had a child. This unfortunate child had become sick after eating an apple and eventually, the child died after three months. Automatically, the blame was placed upon Alke Engels, an eighty-year-old widow.

Without any proof, Engels was accused of being a witch for it was this woman who had given the child an apple about three months ago. It was claimed she must have done some sort of witchcraft on the apple before giving it to the child. After a tortuous interrogation, she was one of the so-called witches who was burned on the hill.

With each execution, the executioner would financially benefit. On top of the execution, the other hard and inhumane aspect was that the relatives of the convicted witches had to pay for all expenses of the execution. In addition, the villagers had to give up one peat after each execution.

Today, on the same hill where the burnings had taken place is a memorial stone. The names of all the known victims are displayed on this stone. The memorial, in honor of the victims, has the following message on top in Dutch:

"Ter herinnering aan een gruwelijke gebeurtenis in Westerwolde."

This message translated to English is:

"In memory of a horrific event in Westerwolde."

Today, as we awaken at dawn and have some herbal tea to help with a cold, we do not have to worry about being accused of witchcraft. The pain and tears of the innocent still roam within the pages of history. Time heals everything. We have crossed enough time to realize we had done unjust.

History cannot be changed but history teaches from the past. The memorial stone sitting on the Geselberg teaches the present generation of the horrific and unjust justice given to the accused witches. Standing in front of the memorial stone, you the present generation shall acknowledge injustice for time retells the stories of the past inhabitants.

Through these stories, we the future learn our lessons where we know just from unjust. Today, the land of the International Court of Justice retells the stories of her past inhabitants. The land of the World Court reminds us the world citizens not to be the judge.

Engels was judged by blindfolded anger, revenge, or ignorance. Yet, the future citizens of her land remember her and her story. Hopefully, this has brought justice to her memories as Alke Engels shall always be remembered from the Netherlands as everblooming.

FATHER OF
THE DELTA WORKS:
JOHAN VAN VEEN

Uithuizermeeden is a small village in Groningen near the Wadden Sea. Here on December 21, 1893, the Dutch hydraulic engineer Johan van Veen was born. The love and bond he had with this land made him into the person he became.

A land where floods ravish homes is a fear all lived with. Yet, through their joint efforts, the Dutch befriended the sea instead of fearing her. Let us travel to the past and walk through the life of a great honorable person who we shall not forget. We shall remember him through his will to save his birthland. His efforts to do something is evidence of a son and his love for his land, sea, and people.

Van Veen is one of the prides of the province of Groningen where he began his journey. He graduated from the Delft University of Technology in 1919. After having different jobs, in 1929, Van Veen began working at the Rijkswaterstaat which is part of the Ministry of Infrastructure and Water Management.

He investigated the Zeeland dikes and water management by the coast. Van Veen would sometimes use a pen name, Dr. Cassandra, in his publications so he could write his ideas freely. According to his investigation in 1937, he shared that the Zeeland dikes would not be able to stand up to major storm surges.

According to Van Veen, the dikes in the southwestern Netherlands were too weak and too low. He believed there could be a dangerous situation if there were to be a storm surge. He faced rejections along the way, but he kept investigating and did not give up.

Reports in the 1930s supporting this idea led way to the establishment of the Stormvloedcommissie (English: Storm Flood Commission) in 1939 and Van Veen was the secretary. He worked on a plan to fill in gaps by connecting the islands in South Holland. By doing so, the coastline would be reduced and all the existing dikes would not have to be raised to be taller than they were.

On January 29, 1953, Van Veen presented a draft Delta Plan. On the night of January 31 to February 1, 1953, the North Sea flooded into Zeeland, South Holland, and North Brabant. The Delta Works was a project to protect the land from floods. The project began quickly after the flood because the Delta Commission was able to incorporate many parts of Van Veen's pre-existing plan. Storm surge barriers, dams, levees, sluices, dikes, and locks were built so that the coastline would be made shorter, all the previous dikes would not have to be raised, and the Rhine–Meuse–Scheldt delta would be protected from flooding.

Van Veen had numerous heart attacks and the final fatal one had come during a train ride in 1959. After his death, it was realized the world had listened to his ideas but was too late as the honorable person did not see his plans come to fruition. His soul, however, finally would find peace as his ideas were used not only for the Delta Works, but also for other projects including the Maasvlakte at the Port of Rotterdam and the Port of Eemshaven in Groningen.

The travelers we all are, trying to complete our journeys through life. We stumble upon huge boulders while trying to go forward. These boulders are at times humans creating a blockage within our lives.

Sometimes, we are able to go forward with a fight. At times, life itself takes a turn as time is not always our friend. For Van Veen, time was his enemy as well as human blockages. He never lost faith.

The irony is even if not in his life, after his death, people would realize the extent of his work. Today, the Dutch are in their safe haven because of this great man's ideas. It matters not if a person only has a short life to live. Van Veen is always here even from the beyond through his blessed ideas. The Dutch are not only helping themselves but have become a saving grace for all the low-lying countries around the globe.

When you again visit the province of Groningen, do know this great man was born here. I believe life is a day. You, the individual, can live for yourself and all others through your give and take of this day. Van Veen lived his life on this Earth within his allocated time.

He was a great man who from the past has become a father all of the Dutch look up to and learn from. Not only had he taught the children of his land but his message has reached the humans who from other nations are trying to find a way to save their lands from the ravishing waters. His given lesson even in his allocated time of life is a saving grace for low-lying nations across this world.

Van Veen made the time to save his land and his people from the ravishing sea even if not in his time. Others would lend him a helping hand from the future to complete what he had started. His idea gifted him the name, Father of the Delta Works, for which the world shall always remember Johan van Veen from the Netherlands as everblooming.

TWIN FLAMES:
SIENTJE AND HENDRIK

Groningen has given birth to so many wonderful children. I would want all of you to come and get acquainted with a proud daughter of this province. As time passes by, what could we the present give the future generations to have as a keepsake for eternity? Some leave their life stories while some leave behind their invention, creation, music, artwork, or just a message from the past. These messages tie their life journeys to the yet to be born humans in the future. Remember, every life has a message as all humans are vessels carrying messages for the future.

Come and let us get acquainted with Sina "Sientje" Mesdag-van Houten, a great woman from the past, a lover, a wife, a mother, and an artist, who left behind her legacy for the future generations. Sientje was born in Groningen on December 23, 1834 into a very wealthy family. Her father had a timber business and was financially well off. As a young woman, she fell in love with her twin flame Hendrik Willem Mesdag and in 1856, they tied the knot. They promised to be together throughout all the ups and downs of life. Hendrik was born on February 23, 1831, also an honorable son of Groningen. He had been working at his father's bank and was able to provide for himself and his wife with his banking job. After work, he spent time on art as it was his favorite hobby.

In 1863, Sientje gave birth to their son Nicolaas "Klaas." Klaas was the only child this couple would have. In 1864, Sientje's father had died, leaving her behind a large inheritance. She had used this inheritance money to help her husband pursue his dream career of being an artist. Sientje loved her husband to an extent that she would do whatever she had to, so he could pursue his goal. Sientje, a twin flame of her husband, knew in love there is no sacrifice but complete willingness.

In 1866, Sientje supported her husband to pursue his path to becoming a painter and quit his banking job. With the financial backing that they now had, they were able to move and Hendrik learned more about art and painting. With her husband, Sientje also experienced the world of art. Her main focus, however, was their son as a mother had awakened within her.

Unfortunately in 1871, their only child passed away. With his passing, Sientje devoted herself in the world of painting. With her husband's support, she took upon her hands another world where she could create through her imagination. Both she and her husband had great success with their paintings. Both had earned numerous awards and participated in exhibitions in other countries, individually and jointly. Their collection of art had grown so much that eventually they no longer had space in their home. They ended up buying the plot next to them, which later became the Mesdag Museum in The Hague.

One of their greatest collaborations was the Panorama Mesdag. In 1879, Hendrik first met a Belgian society, "Société Anonyme du Panorama Maritime de la Haye." In 1880, he was recruited to create the majestic panorama. Panoramas were popular as they were a source of entertainment. Hendrik was able to choose the subject of the painting and with whom he would work. As a marine painter, Hendrik loved the sea. He wanted to create an artwork of Scheveningen that all would be able to see even in the future. Through this painting, he wanted to bridge the gap between the past, present, and future.

The work started on March 28, 1881. After a few months of hard and devoted work, finally the grand opening to view the completed panorama was on August 1, 1881. On his team, he took his wife along with others to produce the largest panoramic painting in Europe at a size of around 46 feet (14 meters) in height and around 395 feet (120 meters) in circumference. One landmark is clearly missing from the panoramic painting, the Kurhaus which would be built a few years later. When Vincent van Gogh visited, he had said, "The Mesdag Panorama is the most beautiful sensation of my life. It has just one tiny flaw and that is its flawlessness."

The panorama company went bankrupt in 1886 but Hendrik bought the building and kept it open for all to visit. This is one of the biggest tourist attractions in The Hague today. You too can walk inside this building and build a bridge of love and appreciation with the past through your love for their paintings.

Sientje, a proud wife and a mother, did not want to be remembered as just Mrs. Mesdag, but an artist and for her work. She from the past had created another door for her future sisterhood of women. Even though after she passed away, she was only remembered as the wife of the marine painter Hendrik, people now acknowledge her as a great painter and an amazing artist.

Within the panorama, Hendrik forever immortalized his wife as a painter. He left an imprint for all future generations to see. Hendrik painted his wife sitting behind an easel, painting on the Scheveningen beach. He wanted his wife to be known to the world as a great painter, a wife, and a mother.

Both were members of the Hague School, a group of painters. In addition to the many awards both received for their paintings, in 1903, Hendrik was honored as Knight Grand Cross in the Order of Orange-Nassau. In 1904, Sientje was honored as Officer in the Order of Orange-Nassau.

A blessed couple, true twin flames, from the past teaches us the lessons of love and partnership. After their child's death, Hendrik helped Sientje get immersed in something. Hendrik helped her become an artist as she had the skills and passion to be one. They loved and supported one another.

Be there for one another and support each other, you the twin flames who on this day are taking the blessed vows of marriage. Life is a blessed journey when you walk for one another with one another as love birds throughout time. Here, a couple equally shared their passion for art and created the Panorama Mesdag. Through this amazing shared talent of a couple, we the future know where there is love and support, there is always a complete creation.

Be it admired by thousands or none, the art of passion travels time as this couple through their art has traveled time. A husband's love and belief in his wife shows partnership in true form. His love for her and her love for him gifted us the artist couple, Sina "Sientje" Mesdag-van Houten and Hendrik Willem Mesdag, as they shall always be from the Netherlands, everblooming.

CHAPTER NINE:

DRENTHE

"Green fields spread throughout the land are serenity for the beloved travelers seeking only peace."

-Ann Marie Ruby

DRENTHE

Come travel with me and let us get acquainted

With some of my past inhabitants.

My land is used for farming

As I have created farmers out of my inhabitants.

I help my country provide food to feed this one world.

You, the admirer of natural landscapes, will be blessed

As your eyes admire my natural landscaping.

I have kept sacredly

The more than five-thousand-year-old tombstones

Known as the hunebedden

To remember my past inhabitants.

Stop by my capital city Assen

And admire the motorcycle racing circuit

With my participating inhabitants.

You shall find me within my country, the Netherlands,

For I am known

As the province

DRENTHE.

In the
northeastern part of
the Netherlands,
is Drenthe.
On her west,
is Friesland.
To her north,
is Groningen.
To her south,
is Overijssel.

Welcome to Drenthe. The capital of this province is Assen. In this province, you are able to enjoy the beautiful countryside. We can trace the inhabitants of this province back to around 150,000 years ago. Some of the oldest artifacts in the Netherlands are found here. The Drents Museum in Assen has kept many artifacts of the past safe. Neolithic stone monuments called hunebedden (English: dolmens) are also found in this province. These are huge tombstones that date back at least five thousand years.

Within this province, you can visit Camp Westerbork. The camp was originally made by the Dutch for Jewish refugees in 1939. When the Nazis took over in 1942, the camp's role changed. The Nazis used the camp to gather Jewish, Roma, and Sinti people. These victims were then deported from Camp Westerbork to concentration camps.

Come, let us visit some of the past inhabitants of Drenthe.

PESSE CANOE OF DRENTHE: HENDRIK WANDERS

During the hot summer nights, a quiet walk in the parks, near the lakes, and the forestlands, is my dream vacation. With bright stars in the night skies, I could escape the crowded tourists and maybe get to visit some inhabitants of the past. Yes, then I would want to go to Drenthe.

Just like humans talk from the past, did you know even objects found from the past talk about their creators and their surroundings? They create a bridge between time. So, remember as you see this object today, you have created a bond to the person who had touched this years ago when it was created.

In 1955, the A28 motorway was being built near the village of Pesse. The crew was clearing out the land and taking out peat when their crane stopped. They found an object and thought it was a tree trunk. This object was more than 6 feet (2 meters) below the ground.

They had the help of a local farmer by the name of Hendrik Wanders. This farmer had realized the object was not a tree trunk and wanted it to get inspected. He had sent this to the University of Groningen. The university had taken this seriously and thereafter a lot of research went into the investigation of the object.

They realized with carbon dating, this canoe was about ten thousand years old. It was created between 8040 BCE and 7510 BCE. A lot of disputes were considered as to whether it really was a functioning canoe. Through the recreation of the canoe, scientists had proven this canoe to indeed be a canoe capable of floating.

The oldest canoe we know of on Earth has found its home in the Drents Museum in Assen, the Netherlands. A local farmer with his insistence has given us the world citizens, our oldest canoe. A person's devotion to his belief and following his intuition rather than other people's criticism has benefitted all of us. It is wise not to be the critic, yet if criticism comes upon our hands, we should be brave and not give up on our beliefs.

Remember, if all unthinking and unknown critics could have their ways, we today would not have these discoveries. We would not have some of our favorite movies, songs, or even books. Critics will criticize, but people like Wanders will be born over and over, maybe with a different name, different face, or maybe in a different land. Today, we the citizens of this world have the Pesse canoe as a gift from a farmer. For his belief, farmer Hendrik Wanders shall be always remembered from the Netherlands as everblooming.

BEACON OF HOPE: JOHANNES POST AND NIEUWLANDE

Nieuwlande, a small Dutch village, glows like the candles of hope. The glowing light of hope takes us back to 1942 and 1943, when World War II had humans hunting for humans. Everywhere, there were frightened children and adults looking for shelter from the hunters.

Where do these victims go and find safety? How do they find food and water in hiding? All of these questions were answered as a village became a shelter. Not one home, or one bunker, but the complete village became the umbrella of protection for the victims. Come let us travel time and see how a village protected these victims.

Johannes Post was a local town councilor and farmer. He came to be known as a great Dutch resistance leader in this village and within the Netherlands. In 1942, Reverend Fredrik "Frits" Slomp spoke to the villagers about the resistance movement. He preached to the church attendees that as Christians, they should help others in need. He asked all to do their human duties first and save all lives, not just Christians.

Everyone in the village would take in one Jewish family or at least one Jewish person. The villagers risked their own lives by taking in Jewish people. Arnold Douwes and Max Nico Léons helped Post with the Dutch resistance movement against the Nazis. Douwes, the son of a pastor, was insistent that villagers help and was instrumental in taking refugees into safe havens. Léons was a young Jewish man himself, but still helped going by his middle name Nico. Albert Nijwening would deliver bread on his bicycle between different communities and assisted in finding hiding places for Jews.

It took the whole village to protect each other and the victims who found refuge within their village. They had to keep their properties safe if Nazi inspectors were to come. As an example, the villagers took off all the house numbers so people unfamiliar with the village would get slowed down. They were all united in this effort to save lives. The villagers knew they were all in it together, so whatever happened, it would happen to all of them.

They made do with whatever or wherever they could hide people in, such as barns or cellars. Even though Post was killed after a courageous attempted raid to save prisoners who were unjustly arrested, his work and his bravery did not go unheard. Because of Post's bravery and leadership, the village of Nieuwlande collectively saved hundreds of people.

After the war, this village was one of the only two villages where all of the villagers collectively received the Righteous Among the Nations award from Yad Vashem for their part in rescuing Jewish victims during World War II. The other one was the French village, Le Chambon-sur-Lignon. A village that collectively saves lives is an example of humans united within strength. One lantern lighting one house will keep the family going through dawn. Yet a village filled with lanterns burning throughout the dark nights, is the beacon of hope for eternity.

Today, through this book, I would like all of you to spread the blessed message of a village that worked for one another, a village that became the beacon of hope for all throughout time. The villagers of Nieuwlande of 1942 and 1943 were recognized for their bravery, courage, and love. This is one such story where I the future had so much wanted to time travel if I only could save Post's life and give my helping hand. Some of our wishes, however, are separated by the mystical time tunnel. Yet through my words,

Johannes Post and his village, Nieuwlande, shall always be remembered, from the Netherlands, as everblooming.

BLESSINGS OF HENDRIKJE VAN ANDEL-SCHIPPER

Drenthe is famously known as the home of fifty-two large hunebedden in the Netherlands. Two more are located in the neighboring province of Groningen. The hunebedden are the oldest burial tombstones found in the Netherlands. The creators of these hunebedden are called the Funnel Beaker people.

Today, I would like all of you to visit a small village in Drenthe called Smilde. Here we will not visit the oldest hunebedden in the country but go on a thirty-five minutes' drive away from the hunebedden to visit an admirable human. This human, with her experience, could teach the world population the lessons of living.

Come meet Hendrikje "Hennie" van Andel-Schipper who was born on June 29, 1890 and lived in the 1800s, 1900s, and 2000s. Let us call her Aunt Hennie as she was called by so many. On February 16, 2001, she was 110 years and 232 days old which made her the oldest living person of the Netherlands. She remained the oldest living person of the Netherlands for the rest of her life.

The journey to life, the gate of entry, and the gate of exit are all the same. The only difference between all of us, the humans, is our chosen path and our actions. Let us get to know this great inspirational woman and her secret path to life and living. Let us find out how she controlled her life and did not let her life control her.

Born prematurely, Aunt Hennie began her war with life at birth, but she was resilient. She had decided she would win this battle as she had her dedication, and willpower to be victorious. Her grandmother's love and support had given her a second chance at life. Aunt Hennie's fight with life continued through her childhood as her health was weak. Her father, a headmaster, homeschooled her. Her mother taught her needlework. She loved theater life and wanted to be an actress, but because her mother did not agree, Aunt Hennie became a handicraft teacher instead.

A teacher chose to teach her subjects because of love. This great woman lived to teach all of us, her students or not. When she was in her forties, Aunt Hennie found the love of her life, Dick van Andel. Her parents, however, did not approve her chosen groom as he was a divorcé. Aunt Hennie had left her parents' home and moved in with a friend, until she eventually married Dick van Andel when she was forty-nine years old in Amsterdam.

The couple had financial difficulties during World War II, but they survived together. Aunt Hennie lost her beloved husband in 1959 to cancer. In 1990, when she was one hundred years old, she too had cancer, but survived after undergoing mastectomy. This strong woman lived independently until she was 105 years old. That is when she moved into a retirement home.

On August 30, 2005, the Netherlands lost a great Dutch citizen as Aunt Hennie had passed away at the age of 115 years and two months. She had given an interview to the Netherlands' RNTV which was featured on *CNN World Report*. Aunt Hennie had said her secrets to her longevity were eating raw herring, drinking a glass of orange juice, and practicing breathing techniques every day. Up to the days nearing her death, she remained alert. The only problems she had were her weakness and deteriorating vision due to age.

She was a strong and determined woman who had lived life her way. Aunt Hennie did not let the obstacles of life be an obstacle for her. She was a woman who lived her life peacefully even through all the hurdles of life. Aunt Hennie had a no worry, be happy attitude toward life. With her life, she is an example of peace and serenity. Before passing away, Aunt Hennie decided to donate her physical body to science, in order to find out how she had lived so long. This was her gift left for all the world citizens. Maybe in life she could not say how she had lived so long, but after her death, scientists can figure out the secrets to longevity.

Here, we have visited a woman who had lived to teach as she was a teacher by profession. Through her life, she lived to teach as her longevity had become a lesson left for us to learn from. Aunt Hennie taught us that life is a lesson learned through living. Even after death, the lessons left by the teacher are studied by her students.

Aunt Hennie lived a happy life as happiness is within one's control. Even after her death, she gifted this world the best-kept secret to living which is being happy. The happiest children in this world come from the same land. Hendrikje "Hennie" van Andel-Schipper will be remembered to the world as the woman who lived to be 115 years old, from the Netherlands, forever everblooming.

CHAPTER TEN:

OVERIJSSEL

"The scenic river IJssel flows along your land and forever frames her memories within the human minds as the ever so beautiful romantic place which houses the village without roads."

-Ann Marie Ruby

OVERIJSSEL

Across the river IJssel, I am.

I am known as the Venice of the Netherlands.

My peace, harmony, and love

Attract you to me and me to you.

I have a village with no roads

Where you can be romantic under the moonlight as

Twin flames find themselves within a canoe in my canals.

My preserved old town center in Kampen,

Has over five hundred monuments,

Which you can visit and learn from

As you keep these found stories as a gift within your soul.

It is within my land, you can find

The clogs village of Enter.

Do go and take a stroll through my capital city Zwolle.

You shall find me within my country, the Netherlands.

I am known

As the province

OVERIJSSEL.

In the
eastern part of
the Netherlands,
is Overijssel.
On her west, is Flevoland.
To her northwest, is Friesland.
To her northeast,
is Drenthe.
To her south and southwest,
is Gelderland.

Welcome to Overijssel. The capital of this province is Zwolle. This province is located across the river IJssel and her largest city is Enschede. Giethoorn, the Dutch Venice, is one of the top chosen vacation stops within this province as her frames will frame your pictures even for your future generations.

Giethoorn has only canals, walking paths, and bike paths. This village is famous for having no roads. Do not forget to take your cameras along with you on this trip. Make a note in your memories to keep them safe for eternity. I could actually live here forever in the memory lane of my travels. When visiting this province, you will get the feeling of being on a dream vacation, a lover's paradise.

Now, let us go on a trip and visit some of this province's past residents.

THE SINGRAVEN ESTATE

Within the province of Overijssel, the Landgoed Singraven (English: Singraven Estate) sits on the river Dinkel. The gorgeous park-like setting has a private watermill, an estate house, and a beautiful garden. The picturesque atmosphere hosts wedding ceremonies where one can bridge time through the setting of the estate. The bride can choose to have a majestic wedding or a countryside wedding, either way a dream wedding for a dream bride.

For the history buffs and those thrilled by horror films, this estate also has a rich history. Within its history, some stories are believed to be true and some are so-called legends. Traveling back in time to the 1500s, this estate was a monastery for around ten years. A legend says at least one of the past inhabitants still roams around the estate. A monastery where the nuns walk with their rosaries, or where Bible recitation is heard, is the peaceful music of the inner soul. Candles flicker as the wind comes blessing all of whom visit or live there.

The legend that has been repeated over time is that this monastery was linked to a sinful and unclean person who had broken her vow. This person was a nun who had taken a vow to be upon the path of the Lord, but her unchaste dealings with the villagers had defamed her reputation eternally. As she had broken her vow, she is said to have been punished severely by the monastery.

As the legend goes, the monastery had bricked her within its walls. After this incident, the nun is said to have been haunting the monastery. Her screams would be heard for a long time. After her screams stopped, her haunting continued through the gardens and the estate.

This haunting of Singraven Estate has been linked to the death of Hendrik Jan Bernhard Roessingh Udink on the same estate. One night in 1878, he had been drinking, and in a freak accident, when he tried to light his cigar, he knocked over his oil lamp and instead lit his long beard. His entire body caught on fire. Udink's employees tried to save him by dumping him directly into the river Dinkel. Although they were able to extinguish the fire, Udink still died because of his injuries.

I do not know if the nun really broke her oath, as she never lived to talk about this. I wonder how a person could have a fair trial if she was bricked up in a wall. If a nun breaks her oath to God, then is it not for God to deal with her sins? My thought always is if you have sinned, then the wagon of karma takes over in this life. The relationship with God is a bond created in Heaven eternally, as we are God's creation. The judgment must be in a worldly court for the worldly sins.

As I always say, "Let us the judged not be The Judge." We will always wonder, did the nun sin? Why is she still haunting? Was she unjustly judged by her fellow nuns? Will her soul find peace?

She was buried within a wall where she cannot even talk from or say her side of the story. If only walls could talk, we always say. Yet here if a nun buried within a wall could say her story, what would she say? The story is hiding within the walls of the Singraven Estate. Some call this nun story a legend, yet the story of Udink is said not to be a legend but an actual event that had taken place.

The past inhabitants who had gone through unfortunate events tell a story of karma. If Udink was not drunk, his beard would not have caught fire to the extent of causing his death. If the nun had broken her vow, she should have been allowed to leave for it takes a great vow, determination, and honor to become a nun. Not everyone can take this path.

The past inhabitants of the Singraven Estate stand tall like a warning sign on a major highway, signaling what roads we should avoid through our journey of life. The Singraven Estate, from her past, gives us lessons for which we the students will keep her as a teacher from the Netherlands, always everblooming.

POET'S JOURNEY: JOHANNA VAN BUREN

The river IJssel flows along this province, spreading her peace and serenity to the inhabitants of this land. The singing birds flying all over Giethoorn, the Venice of the Netherlands, create a beautiful dreamland. All come here to make their dreams into reality. Here, we find the sunsets and the amazing sunrises are framed not only within portraits but words too.

Come and let us visit a place called Hellendoorn, where families go to visit the Avonturenpark Hellendoorn (English: Adventure Park Hellendoorn). I hope you all have had an adventurous day at this park. Now, I want you all to come with me and travel back in time to 1881.

Come and meet Johanna Frederika van Buren who was born on December 20, 1881. Before the age of two, she had lost her father. Van Buren grew up with her brother and their mother.

From a young age, she knew how to establish herself financially as she became a seamstress. She knew this was a talent she could teach all young girls and they too would have this talent which would always be theirs. When her mother passed away, Van Buren found employment at the post office.

Her love for all things her eyes would see became a passion as she picked up her pen and paper. Within a day, we, the humans, have so many different forms of passion, anger, and personal memories we walk through. Van Buren had placed these feelings down on paper as poetry.

When she was forty-five years old, she started to publish her poems in the local dialect in the newspaper. She knew the people around her too wanted to express their feelings through her words. Everyone could relate with her simple words of love and looked forward to reading her words every week. We, the humans, feel the same grief and the same sorrow. Our tears are all the same color as are our feelings of love and joy. Van Buren found her fans had related to her as they waited every week for her poem to appear in the newspaper.

So much love and blessings her poems had found within all of the readers, but all had wondered whether she found love in her life. She never married and remained single even on her deathbed. Yet, it is said she did find love as she had written about love within her poems.

Words have tied a bond with all of whom had picked up Van Buren's poetry. The love that she had within her inner soul remains as a gift for this world. She is an amazing poet this world will have for eternity, through her gifts left behind. Van Buren physically left this world on January 17, 1962, at a retirement home. She is remembered even after her death. As a tribute to Van Buren, on the day she would have turned one hundred years old in 1981, a collection of a thousand of her poems was published in *Verzamelde gedichten.*

Today as an author, I would want to say my dream is to be loved like her. The words of an author are all her love for this world. An author has nothing in between her beloved readers and her words. Always the poems, stories, prayers, or even quotes written are only for the ones reciting them.

In the final journey of these words, they find their owners. No author holds on to her works as they are gifts for the receivers. Each person holding the book is the owner of this gift. When you recite them, you should know they are emotions written for you, and only you. Gifts from an author travel time, as within this journey, the books and all the words become immortal.

Van Buren was a great poet who should never be forgotten as her words will always be remembered throughout time. Within her land and her people, she still lives. Through this book, may her story reach all throughout this world. Johanna Frederika van Buren, an author and a poet, from the Netherlands, throughout time will be known as everblooming.

THE SPEAKING LANDSCAPES OF HENDRICK AVERCAMP

The province of Overijssel is known to all as the home of Giethoorn, yet a little over 24 miles (39 kilometers) away is a small city called Kampen. Here, I would want all of you to take a short break and travel time with me to the years 1585 to 1634. During this time period, another great painter had lived. He left behind an admirable legacy through his life lived. Let us visit this painter, Hendrick Avercamp.

He was born in Amsterdam into a wealthy family. Avercamp and his family moved to Kampen where his father was employed as the town apothecary, similar to what we would call a pharmacist today. After his father died, his mother and one of his brothers managed the family business. Another brother had become a physician.

Avercamp was known as "de Stomme van Kampen" (English: "the Mute of Kampen"). He was mute and may have also been deaf. Avercamp, however, picked up the colors of life through his artist's palette, brush, watercolors, and a canvas. Through his imagination, he had brought to life the landscapes of this world. He was a landscape painter.

In particular, he painted winter landscapes. He is thought to have been taught by Pieter Isaacsz in Amsterdam.

His mother, Beatrix Peters, was worried about his life. The world is a big place where life and people do not always find justice. She had willed that after her death, her son should inherit one hundred guilders every year on top of what he would inherit. The great painter would live only for five months more after her will was written. As fate would have it, the son passed away before the mother.

The death of this great painter did not stop him from becoming one of the most famous landscape painters of the seventeenth century. Without any voice or sound, he still talks to all as he framed this world within his canvas. The artist and his paintings live eternally through his art. The footprints and the beholders of the footprints on the sand are washed away by the waves of time. Although people and landscapes may change, within Avercamp's portraits, the people and the landscapes are immortal upon the walls of museums.

Life is a journey where we the travelers change, as there were people before us and there shall be people after us. Travelers like Avercamp, however, unite all travelers through their devoted gifts to this world. A mother's worry about her son's life, was answered through his devoted paintings as they live on to this day.

Within his canvases, he not only painted but spread hope from the past to the future. Avercamp shall always be remembered as the great phrase says, "Where there's a will, there's a way." He found his way from the past to the future to speak with all through his framed canvases. For this, the landscape painter Hendrick Avercamp from the Netherlands shall always be everblooming.

CHAPTER ELEVEN:

GELDERLAND

"History, the teacher, is forever present within the footsteps of the past. Remember we can greet and learn from this teacher as we revisit the tales of the past."

-Ann Marie Ruby

GELDERLAND

Memories of my past inhabitants come

And give historical lessons on the fields of my land.

Here, I have kept history alive

As history teaches all from the past.

Nijmegen is one of the oldest cities in my country,

Where you too can witness history.

The famous Battle of Arnhem had taken place here

In my capital city of Arnhem.

Do come and see if the historical battle can teach

You, the present, how you can avoid all wars.

Do stop by the famous Paleis Het Loo

Which was once a royal residence.

Today, you can still feel like a royal

As you visit the famous museum.

Do stop by my country and visit me

As within my country, the Netherlands, I am known

As the province

GELDERLAND.

175

In the
eastern part of
the Netherlands, is Gelderland.
On her west,
are Utrecht and South Holland.
To her north and northwest, is
Flevoland.
To her north and northeast,
is Overijssel.
To her south are North Brabant
and Limburg.

Welcome to Gelderland, the largest province in the Netherlands in terms of land. The capital city of this province is Arnhem. Gelderland was named after the German town Geldern which is nearby. There is a story that states the Lords of Pont had killed a dragon around 878 AD. The dragon had said, "Gelre! Gelre!" while dying, and this is where the names Geldern and hence Gelderland come from.

The famous Paleis Het Loo (English: Het Loo Palace) is in this province. This had been Queen

Wilhelmina's summer home and where she lived after she abdicated. Het Loo Palace is now a state museum, however, members of the Dutch Royal Family do still reside on the estate. Het Loo House was built on the estate for Princess Margriet and her husband Pieter van Vollenhoven Jr. Her husband was the first commoner to become a member of the Dutch Royal House.

This province also has within her chest, the memories of the Battle of Arnhem, a major battle during World War II. In the Arnhem Oosterbeek War Cemetery, there are 1,764 graves of World War II victims. As more victims are discovered, their bodies are brought here. The famous John Frostbrug (English: John Frost Bridge) is also within this province.

Let us now go and visit the past inhabitants of this province. Time separates us from them. Through the pages of a book, we can be there in that place and time and see them from our time yet their future. Come with me as I take you to the past.

SILENT WITNESS: HUIS BINNENVELD

Huissen is a town in Gelderland by the rivers Nederrijn and Linge. This town has a story that she has witnessed and shared with the world. Let us travel to the past and see for ourselves what had taken place within this town before we enter a very famous house.

This town and her residents were witnesses to the horrors of World War II. Huissen because of her location, witnessed the battles that took place in Arnhem and Nijmegen. On October 2, 1944, the town of Huissen was severely damaged because of the war and over 150 people in the town had lost their lives. Because of limited material for coffins and lack of time, most of the deceased were placed in a mass grave.

The memories of war haunt the restless souls, their families, friends, and all of whom have witnessed war firsthand. These memories continue to haunt those who shall witness across time from the future. The pain never dies, even though the victims pass on.

Let us now go and enter a house which had withstood the war and has witnessed horrific happenings. Yet, this house cannot speak or retell the stories that haunt her. The past inhabitants, however, can speak through their spiritual presence.

Standing within the horrendous war scenes in the town of Huissen was Huis Binnenveld. This is a historic house which was built in 1735 on what was originally a farming estate from the sixteenth century. A beautiful home she is, but the memories she holds within her chest are painful.

She is the last standing witness to these memories. Some of these stories have been kept alive as they have been spoken of throughout time. Hundreds of years ago, in the 1700s, she was unable to give protection to people seeking shelter from a flood. Through the years, she has witnessed women hanging themselves within her attic.

During World War II, she witnessed soldiers die in front of her. All of these stories are buried within her, but the house still came up on the market for sale numerous times. She told her buyers she was not at fault for the unwelcome guests that reside within her walls.

The house has passed hands several times recently. Paranormal investigators have visited the house to see if the house is haunted. Different groups of paranormal investigators have entered this house to try and see if they could help the past inhabitants. Some have said they felt the presence of the past inhabitants and some have said they could not determine either way.

Perhaps it is up to the past inhabitants if they want to show themselves or not. At times, it is up to the individuals to decide for themselves if they would like to believe or not believe. If only we could ask the house and if only she could tell us her side, but we cannot. So, it is up to our minds to take us on a journey through history that only lives within the past.

A new owner bought the property, renovated it, and made apartments within it. In 2019, the apartments were completed. Huis Binnenveld is a national monument. To the locals though, this house is still known as the haunted house of Huissen.

This house has had a lot of owners who have not wanted to live in the house because of her past residents. So, it is understandable that the owners of this historical house have changed throughout the years. How could one blame him or herself for not wanting to live in a haunted house where people may still see a woman who hung herself?

People still witness the pain and screams of the soldiers of World War II. A home is where love and peace blossom. A home is a place you want to rest your mind, body, and soul within. This world is a temporary home for you are the guests who arrive at birth and depart at death.

I wonder though, what about the residents who have somehow missed their flights back home? How would they get on the next flight available to them? Yes, these residents have missed their flights and are unwelcome, unpaid guests, at the houses they once owned, resided in, or visited.

Let us all the travelers of today, pay some respect to the past. We can try to see if we the living can help the past travelers. Let us show them their way back home by showing them they are not feared. Their action is or was maybe feared, but not them. Let them be in peace as we the present live in peace.

This house is proof that all the soldiers or victims of any war should never be forgotten. We should keep their memories alive just like this house wants to keep the memories of the past innocent inhabitants alive through her memories. All memories of the past inhabitants and all the victims who witnessed the horrific events of World War II across this historical house, Huis Binnenveld, from the Netherlands, shall be everblooming.

SECRET BOOK CHEST OF HUGO DE GROOT

The Slot Loevestein (English: Loevestein Castle), is a water castle built sometime between 1357 and 1397. Later in 1619, this castle became a prison for political prisoners. Let us go and visit a famous political prisoner, a humanist, an eminent lawyer, a poet, a theologian, and a politician. He had published his first book in 1599 when he was only sixteen years old, *Martiani Minei Felicis Capellæ Carthaginiensis viri proconsularis Satyricon.*

The world knows the political prisoner as Hugo Grotius, or Hugo de Groot. A person who the world would admire through his works left for the humans, had become a political prisoner. A religious conflict in 1610 had resulted in Stadholder-Prince Maurice and De Groot to take different sides. Because of these differences, in 1619, the famous humanist, De Groot, became a political prisoner and had begun his life imprisonment in Loevestein Castle.

His wife Maria van Reigersberch was an independent and intellectual woman. She was a huge supporter of her husband. Van Reigersberch would have books filled within a chest brought for him regularly. All the prison guards knew of his reading and writing habits, so they had become less suspicious.

On one such occasion in 1621, Van Reigersberch and her maid Elselina van Houwening had brought in another chest for his reading pleasures. Yet, this chest was empty and with the help of his wife and her maid, the political prisoner had fled within the chest. De Groot had escaped to France where he continued his writing career. His family had joined him in France.

Eventually, he became the Swedish Ambassador to France in 1634 as he was liked by the King of Sweden. De Groot passed away in Rostock, Germany on August 28, 1645. His contribution to international law had given him the honor of being known as the "Father of Modern International Law."

His remains were brought back to the Netherlands and he was buried in the Nieuwe Kerk (English: New Church) in Delft even though he was not a part of the Royal Family. Interestingly, Stadholder-Prince Maurice is also buried in the New Church. There are two chests claiming to be the one De Groot had escaped within. One is in Delft in Museum Prinsenhof (English: The Prince's Court Museum), which was the residence of William the Silent where he was also assassinated. The other one is in the Rijksmuseum (English: National Museum) in Amsterdam.

Today, there is a monument of De Groot in front of the New Church. As you visit this monument of a humanist, do remember he stood alone, yet alone for what he believed to be the right path. He may have been lonely during his time, but he certainly is not alone throughout time. On this path after him, there will always be others who will walk.

The path is what we must stand upon, not behind the travelers, but be the traveler you believe in. An honorable humanist De Groot was, and his lessons are our path and guidance to remember always. Guiding throughout time are humans who shall never be forgotten. Hugo de Groot is one such person from the Netherlands who shall always be everblooming.

BLESSED BREAD OF ANTOON OOMEN

On a cold star-filled night, there is no sound, nothing to see, but the smell of fresh-baked bread fills the mind, body, and inner spirit. Share fresh-baked bread with your neighbors and know this neighborly friendship will last forever. Today, I want all of you to come and take a trip with me to a village. This village is called De Horst and it is located in the province of Gelderland.

On May 9, 1906, Antoon Oomen was born into the family of a blacksmith. He married Anna Maria van Balkom, and they lived in De Horst, Gelderland. He was a baker and had a bakery in the village. During World War II, an interesting story emerged from the village of De Horst. This was a land which had been liberated by the Allied troops on September 17, 1944.

Yet a few days later, the German troops came back, and the village was once again a war zone. As all the people tried to find shelter, they found blessings from a monastery. There was a local convent led by Franciscan nuns who helped hide over four hundred villagers within their cellar for four weeks.

During the four weeks while his fellow villagers hid in the nearby cellar, Oomen spent the nights baking bread for his fellow humans. He baked during the nights so no one would see the smoke. He did not do this for money. Humanity overruled all of his fear and he risked his own life to help others.

Although a baker, during the war, he helped with first aid. He was director of the First Aid Association, and after the war, he was group commander of the local Red Cross. For his honorable work with first aid, on May 22, 1969, the Red Cross awarded him with the Silver Merit Medal.

After everything had settled down, Oomen and his beloved wife moved to Milsbeek and then to Breedeweg. Oomen had died at the age of seventy-three in a traffic accident. He is buried in his favorite place on Earth, in De Horst.

A blessed soul had lived not only for himself but his human family friends. He did not allow differences to take over basic humanity. Race, color, and religion only matter when there is no humanity left. When and where there is humanity, heroes like Oomen appear.

Love your fellow humans and do not allow differences to create a bridge of separation amongst you.

Create the bridge of mercy, forgiveness, and blessings for then, across this globe, we shall find stories like Oomen cross over the wagon of time and live on forever. The empowering life story of Antoon Oomen from the Netherlands shall always be everblooming.

CHAPTER TWELVE:

LIMBURG

"From your highest point, you unite three countries through your amazing landscape, creating art to remember throughout all the lands you have united."

-Ann Marie Ruby

LIMBURG

My hills welcome you

As I have the tripoint within my land.

Here three countries can be viewed at the same time,

As you stand on the Vaalserberg,

The highest point in my country.

Within my chest,

I had witnessed the historical Maastricht Treaty in 1992.

My inhabitants bake the best pie, the vlaai,

Which is shared with the visitors of my land.

Do come, sit, relax, and enjoy your pie

In one of the oldest cities in my country,

My capital city, Maastricht.

You shall find me and all of my inhabitants

In my country, the Netherlands,

For I am known

As the province

LIMBURG.

In the
most southeastern
part of
the Netherlands,
is Limburg.
On her west,
is North Brabant.
To her north,
is Gelderland.

Welcome to Limburg. The capital of this province is
Maastricht. The Vaalserberg is the highest point in the
Netherlands. At this point, the three European countries, the
Netherlands, Belgium, and Germany meet. Limburg finds
her name from the neighboring Belgian town Limbourg-sur-
Vesdre. Through the Treaty of London in 1839, Belgium
was separated from the Dutch Limburg and Belgium's
independence was recognized.

During World War II, the residents of Limburg had
actively hidden their Jewish neighbors. In 1992, the famous

treaty, the Maastricht Treaty was signed in this capital for which the European Union was born. This province also is home to the famous city, Roermond, where the biggest witch trial in the Netherlands took place.

Let us now go back in time where we can introduce ourselves to some of the past inhabitants and take a look at their life stories. The only way we the present can connect with the past is through history.

THE LAST WITCH OF KASTEEL LIMBRICHT: ENTGEN LUYTEN

Kasteel Limbricht (English: Limbricht Castle) sits on an artificial hill in a moat. It is an island that looks like a dream palace, a perfect wedding venue where pictures make memories throughout time. These days, couples come to take their sacred vows at this picturesque castle.

Come with me and let us travel time to another century when this castle had held a prisoner. In 1674, the widow of Jacobus Boven die Erdt, Entgen Luyten was captured and imprisoned in the dungeon of the Limbricht Castle. She was accused of witchcraft and magic.

She had a long trial while being kept a prisoner. The prosecutor requested Luyten to be tied on the rack. The rack is a wooden structure that was used to inflict a lot of pain on a prisoner to get a confession. Numerous accusations were brought as a lot of people testified against her. One charge was she had caused an innkeeper, Gorten van Neusz, to die because she had sipped from the same cup before him.

Another charge was that Luyten made Aleth Bruggen crippled so Bruggen could not walk. Yet, after Luyten gave Bruggen bread and salt, Bruggen recovered. Luyten was also blamed for the death of cows. She denied all of the charges and pleaded for her innocence but to no avail. On October 9, 1674, Luyten was found dead in the dungeon with a noose on her neck. The coroner had hinted that it could have been murder. Yet, the reports had declared it to be suicide.

Injustice to another soul had taken place. Where were the humans with humanity? To this day, the victim seeks justice. The famous castle has been on the news for various ghost hunters and various researchers who have visited to decode the mystery of the castle. They have tried to see if they can find peace for the last accused witch who died. Based on their investigation and the experiences of people in the castle, the castle may indeed be haunted but not in a scary or bad way.

It is a tragedy how people could call a person a witch based on the charges that were presented. Even today, we the humans sometimes point our fingers to others without any substantial evidence. The past inhabitants roam around the pages of history not to haunt, but to teach us not to repeat history.

The witch burnings occurred all around Europe and even spread to the United States of America. This was a time period where injustice found its place in the pages of history.

Let the last witch trial in the Netherlands be a message to this world that we will not repeat another unjust justice, for now the Netherlands is the land of peace as she is the home of the Peace Palace. To spread peace, keep peace alive, and not repeat unjust history, Entgen Luyten's life story from the Netherlands shall be remembered as everblooming.

AESTHETIC ARCHITECTURE OF PIERRE CUYPERS

Roermond, a city in the province of Limburg, is famous for the witch trials and witch burning history. Although time gives us some terrifying memories, time also gifts us with iconic humans, whose life journeys gift us treasures which last throughout time. There was a man of Roermond whose visions walk us through the iconic buildings of today.

Today, Amsterdam, Roermond, The Hague, Utrecht, Maastricht, Eindhoven, Alkmaar, Leeuwarden, and Hilversum are only some of the cities with the touch of this architect, in addition to cities in Belgium and Norway. It is hard to envision these cities without this architect's visual influences. Come let us travel to a time when his aesthetic architecture was not appreciated by all, yet the critics did not prevent his visons from completion.

Petrus Josephus Hubertus "Pierre" Cuypers was born in Roermond to Johannes Hubertus Cuypers, and Maria Joanna Bex, on May 16, 1827. The young Cuypers had grown up in the company of his father who was a church painter. A child who looks up to his father never forgets his

197

admiration. This upbringing had influenced and made him into the architect he had become.

Cuypers studied architecture at the Royal Academy of Fine Arts in Antwerp, Belgium. While in Antwerp, in 1850, he married Maria Rosalia van de Vin. In 1851, he got a job as town architect, in Roermond. Cuypers' first work as the town architect was restoring a local church. He had with him his architectural education and his love for art to complete his wish list.

Cuypers and his wife were blessed with two daughters; however, their love would be short-lived as his wife and one of their daughters would die from tuberculosis in 1855. After this devastation, love would give him another chance in life. In 1859, he married Antoinette Catharine Thérèse Alberdingk "Nenny" Thijm. They would have five children—three daughters and two sons. Cuypers was blessed and extremely happy to have met his second wife. It turned out she was a very good singer, so he designed a piano and musical cabinet and gave them to his wife as wedding presents.

Over the years through his career, he designed over one hundred churches and built around seventy churches. His talents were appreciated even beyond his own land.

Cuypers restored many buildings such as De Haar Castle in Haarzuilens and the Ridderzaal (English: Hall of Knights) in The Hague. He also designed the throne in the Ridderzaal in 1904. His architecture had a neo-Gothic design. In 1865, Cuypers had moved to Amsterdam.

He had two big projects in Amsterdam, for which he is renowned. One was the Amsterdam Centraal Station (English: Amsterdam Central Station) and the other one was the Rijksmuseum. He started working on the Rijksmuseum in 1876. The museum opened in 1885. Onlookers even to this day admire the museum's Renaissance and Gothic styles.

Work on the Amsterdam Central Station continued from 1881 to 1889 when the station finally opened. This station also had both Renaissance and Gothic styles. The Rijksmuseum was renovated recently in 2013, bringing back concepts from Cuypers' original architectural plan.

The famous architect had won numerous awards for his work throughout his life. An extraordinarily successful architect he was, even though not everyone appreciated his work. King William III had refused to enter the Rijksmuseum as he complained it looked too much like a cathedral. It was Cuypers' childhood upbringing as a

Catholic that had brewed within him his artistic talents and gave him his love for cathedral styles.

This great architect had left us physically March 3, 1921, in Roermond. Even after his passing, he is still with us as we enter the Central Station in Amsterdam, or visit the largest castle, or the largest museum in the Netherlands. Today, we appreciate his legacy through his amazing architectural details within all of his work.

Life is a journey where we the present are united with the past inhabitants through their left legacies. The high tides of a sea wipe off all the footprints left on the sand, except the gifts of the past left for the future generations. Petrus Josephus Hubertus "Pierre" Cuypers, a loving son from the Netherlands, through his legacy, shall be everblooming.

ROERMOND WITCH TRIALS

The province of Limburg, with its highest point in the Netherlands, has her beautiful green hills, and the smell of fresh-baked vlaai welcoming all of her visitors. The tripoint hill, Vaalserberg, joins her neighboring countries and spreads the warmth of this pie as they too enjoy baking this treat. Within around fifty-five minutes, you can drive into Roermond.

Here, you can go have a fun shopping experience at one of the biggest outlet shopping centers in the Netherlands, called Designer Outlet Roermond. The shopping center attracts visitors from three countries because of its setting in the tripoint area. After the full day, do take a break at sunset, and listen to another story from the past inhabitants of Roermond.

The beautiful countryside of this city carries another side to her history. This part of history binds the world together. This bond, we are not proud of. Throughout Europe, we heard the same screams and cries that crossed the borders and landed within the United States of America. The screams and cries were heard but not the pain and suffering of these victims. Justice was proclaimed by the courts, but the outcome screamed injustice. Let us the present in union remember these victims by retelling some of their stories, and just maybe through this, they too will find peace.

In the cold chilling year of 1613, the largest witch trial in the Netherlands had persecuted sixty-four victims by burning in Roermond. How did we get to this stage, where a judgment was based completely on religious faith? In 1613, Roermond had a great plague. Its inhabitants had proclaimed the plague was a punishment to the city by God because there were witches living amongst them.

The start of the largest witch trial and all of these burnings were credited to a child who was twelve years old. Yes, a child was forced to confess she too was a witch. What would a child say when she is being tortured in the most horrific way possible? She confessed to what they wanted to hear. Is it then her fault? Does she bear the burden of the sin or is she a victim and an innocent soul who cries for the victims she might have innocently sent to the stake? We need to travel time and find out how and when Roermond and her citizens started this tradition.

In 1484, Heinrich Kramer, a German clergyman, had tried to accuse and burn a woman at the stake claiming she was a witch. He was not victorious as the bishop had disagreed to his terms, believing he was crazy. Kramer pursued his unjust belief. To gain more support, he had asked Pope Innocent VIII for help. The Pope had then issued a papal bull on December 5, 1484, that finally gave him power to investigate the witches.

Even with this papal bull, he did not gather much support. In the years 1486 to 1487, Kramer authored his book, *Malleus Maleficarum* (English: Hammer of Witches). This book was based on witches and how to persecute them. He claimed witches were heretic criminals as their actions went against his religious doctrine. Kramer had placed witches on the unjust weighing scales of the predetermined judgment proclaimed by his belief.

Highly educated theologians did not agree with his views. Even then, Kramer won as accused witches were burned at the stake through fear tactics. He had brought his belief of witches and how to persecute them on to all through the power of pen and paper, his book, and the papal bull.

Now let us travel to the year 1522, to the first recorded witch trial of Roermond. From then, the accused witches were burned at the stake. The biggest witch trial was in 1613. It all began as any peasant could bring in his or her charges. This system progressed as later only church and government officials could bring in charges against anyone. People would accuse neighbors if their cows and pigs were harmed, or if their crops were damaged. They would bring in accusations against whomever they could charge. The accusers would prove the guilt of the accused with their powerful voice of the wrongful mouth.

In 1613, a twelve-year-old child was forcibly made to confess she was a witch. In fear of the punishments or maybe out of extreme pain due to the punishments given, she had confessed. Her mother's name was Tryntjen van Zittaert. The child had confessed she had learned magic tricks from her mother. She was charged of being able to make things appear out of her mouth.

Today, we pay a hefty amount of money to watch a magician perform similar tricks. These days, if a child can perform magic tricks, we will welcome this as a learned talent and an amazing skill of art. Time has changed and so has our thinking process. Yet in 1613, the fear the child must have acquired, after the tortured confession or even before the so-called confession for being talented, is beyond today's human comprehension. The mother of this talented child was burned alive and the daughter was imprisoned, supposedly, in a monastery for the rest of her living life.

There was no justice given to the victims, as it was easier to prove their guilt than their innocence. After the horrific sixty-four witch burnings, there were four more burnings between 1614 through 1616 in Roermond. The injustice stopped as we the humans had opened our eyes to fairness and justice. Justice finally found her home in the land of the International Court of Justice, as time and tide had come and brought us to the present time.

Although time passes by, the memories of the past inhabitants remain steadfast through their cries for justice. Today, neighbors in Limburg watch out for one another as they share their baked vlaai in peace. Remember time teaches us through the lives of our past inhabitants. Mistakes are made by us, the humans, even though it is we the humans, who must stand up in union for one another.

The past generations are our past and the future generations are our future. You personally do not have to be the father or mother of the child, as we the society in union raise our villages, our land, and this world together, for we are then one for all, and all for one. The Roermond Witch Trials were during a horrific time in history which we can bring justice to by not repeating. May the memories of the innocent victims of the Roermond Witch Trials from the Netherlands, be within all hearts, everblooming.

CONCLUSION:

EVERBLOOMING

"The sun sets after a long day but comes back as the sun rejuvenates at dawn. Life too ends, but memories rejuvenate throughout time as they are everblooming."

-Ann Marie Ruby

EVERBLOOMING:
THROUGH THE TWELVE PROVINCES
OF THE NETHERLANDS

I danced through the tulip fields and knew

Why flower fields awaken with hope

In Noord-Holland.

Peace found me as I stood and

Tied a ribbon on the wishing tree at the Vredespaleis

In Zuid-Holland.

Where land and water kiss,

And befriend all visitors as they bathe in the sun,

Was reality not a dream I realized as I landed

In Zeeland.

I found the birthplace of the famous painter and

Appreciated the landscape that must have inspired him

In Noord-Brabant.

The weighing scales of Oudewater smiled and told all

She believes in peace and justice

As I met her

In Utrecht.

Smelling like the fresh spring flower,

I stood on the Noordoostpolder

In Flevoland.

I spoke to you in West Frisian

As I sailed within the Wadden Sea

In Friesland.

My admiration for my fellow humans awakened,

As I saw the beautiful human-made landscapes

In Groningen.

Like the flying dove,

I prayed for the more than

Five-thousand-year-old past inhabitants,

As I landed within your green fields and the hunebedden

In Drenthe.

Dreams became a reality when I found myself in a canoe,

Wishing upon a star

In Overijssel.

I rested within a medieval castle as I ended up

In Gelderland.

Amazed I was as I saw the corner,

Where three countries meet

In Limburg.

Stories from beneath your lands awakened my inner soul.

For this, my eternal love for you has woven your memories

As your tales are within my eyes,

EVERBLOOMING:

THROUGH THE TWELVE PROVINCES

OF THE NETHERLANDS.

EVERBLOOMING

The day ends at sunset leaving all in the dark. We the humans lose hope, but we should remember the night stars are all up in the skies guiding us throughout time. Do not forget the bright sun for he shall come back again with new hope, a new name, and in a new form.

Even though we miss the past generation who guided us, there will be a new generation again to guide us. Unrequited lovers, twin flames, painters, inventors, scientists, writers, diarists, humanitarians, accused witches and historical figures all will appear again. Do pay attention to the blinking lights within the sky that tell us the stories of these everblooming bright stars.

The past continues to live through the reactions of their actions. The Netherlands is a small European country with a rich history. The purpose of this book is to keep the inhabitants of this book alive through your acceptance of them. A story never ends as it is retold time after time.

The inhabitants of this book are like human lanterns who glow from their own chapters, always sending their life stories to you as a guide. Learn from their mistakes. Pay attention to their inventions, to their sacrifices, or their dedication as you would to a teacher's journal.

Walk into the homes of these past inhabitants. Pick up their sacrifices, see through their eyes, do not repeat where they have wronged, and learn to change yourself into a better human. See if you too can improve your own land, people, and culture.

Life begins at birth and ends at death. This is true, but through the pages of a book, life lives on. Here, there is no beginning or end for all you have to do is open the pages to the lives of the past, and there in front of you, they are. The past inhabitants never left us as they are all, within the pages of a book, alive.

Each person on this Earth has a gift he or she leaves behind at his or her departure. Their lessons of life make them eternal. As we begin our journey, someone's journey comes to an end. It is like how you wait your turn for the roller coaster. As you get on it, another person's journey comes to an end. Yet, the pictures taken or the memories they have shared about their journey make them and their journey eternal.

As a child, I had retold to all how I loved being on a merry-go-round. I kept the memories alive even though my trip within the fairground had ended. Forever, my first merry-go-round ride stayed within my memories.

Dawn comes as the sun peeks through the night skies and the day ends as the sun sets for the day. The only thing that remains from the day are memories. Like the sun, life too comes to an end; however, through the pages of history, the memories are kept alive throughout time.

In this blessed book, I have shared the stories of some people who have taken their leave like the setting sun. Yet through memories, I have brought them back within the pages of this book. Through their actions of life, we have all sorts of reactions. These reactions are what keep them alive. Like *The Diary of a Young Girl* by Anne Frank, she is still a child retelling her stories. All of these people have something to give to us. We should accept their blessed gifts.

Through this book, I too wanted to give you some Dutch children who with their life stories have given us inspiration, education, romance, and retold not to fear the ghosts of yesteryears. Like a glowing lantern, they are glowing. You can keep their stories glowing. We can build a bridge of love, mercy, forgiveness, and blessings eternally through our shared memories of these souls.

All you have to do is keep their memories alive through the pages of this book by passing this book on throughout time. Let the stories not be lost or forgotten as throughout time, more stories will be written through the lives lived. Then, you the holder of this book can place it in your library of stories not to be forgotten.

This book is your copy of the lives I believe should not be forgotten but kept,

Everblooming:
Through The Twelve Provinces
Of The Netherlands

ABOUT THE AUTHOR

Ann Marie Ruby is an international number-one bestselling author. She has been the unknown face to all her readers throughout her eleven books. The bond between her readers and herself has been created through her eleven books. You have all respected her privacy as she wanted to remain private, never questioned about her pictures, yet gave her your complete love without judging.

Some of you, the reviewers, had gone to the point where you too completely understood her request to remain private. The blessed readers around the globe have made Ann Marie's books bestsellers internationally. She has become from your love, an international number-one bestselling author.

This love that you have poured to an unknown author has awakened her inner self and she wants to give you her gift and reveal her face to this world. So, on the publication of her twelfth book, she would love to be the known face giving you her blessings throughout time. All of you can see Ann Marie on her website and her social media pages. For all of you the readers, she has finally revealed herself.

If this world would have allowed, she would have distributed all of her books to you with her own hands as a gift and a message from a friend. She has taken pen to paper to spread peace throughout this Earth. Her sacred soul has found peace within herself as she says, "May I through my words bring peace and solace within your soul."

As many of you know, Ann Marie is also a dream psychic and a humanitarian. As a dream psychic, she has correctly predicted personal and global events. Some of these events have come true in front of us in the year 2020. She has also seen events from the past. You can read more about her journey as a dream psychic in *Spiritual Lighthouse: The Dream Diaries Of Ann Marie Ruby* which many readers have said is "the best spiritual book" they have read. As a humanitarian, she has taken pen to paper to end hate crimes within *The World Hate Crisis: Through The Eyes Of A Dream Psychic*.

To unite all race, color, and religion, following her dreams, Ann Marie has written two religiously unaffiliated prayer books, *Spiritual Songs: Letters From My Chest* and *Spiritual Songs II: Blessings From A Sacred Soul*, which people of all faiths can recite.

216

Ann Marie's writing style is known for making readers feel as though they have made a friend. She has written four books of original inspirational quotations which have also been compiled in one book, *Spiritual Ark: The Enchanted Journey Of Timeless Quotations.*

As a leading voice in the spiritual space, Ann Marie frequently discusses spiritual topics. As a spiritual person, she believes in soul families, reincarnation, and dreams. For this reason, she answers the unanswered questions of life surrounding birth, death, reincarnation, soulmates and twin flames, dreams, miracles, and end of time within her book *Eternal Truth: The Tunnel Of Light.* Readers have referred to this book as one of the must-read and most thought-provoking books.

The Netherlands has been a topic in various books by Ann Marie. As a dream psychic, she constantly has had dreams about this country before ever having any plan to visit the country or any previous knowledge of the contents seen within her dreams. Ann Marie's love and dreams of the Netherlands brought her to write *The Netherlands: Land Of My Dreams* which became an overnight number-one bestseller and topped international bestselling lists. Now, she brings for this country, *Everblooming: Through The Twelve*

Provinces Of The Netherlands, a keepsake for all generations to come.

You have her name and know she will always be there for anyone who seeks her. Ann Marie's home is Washington State, USA, yet she travels all around the world to find you, the human with humanity. Aside from her books, she loves writing blog posts and articles openly on her website. Through this journey, she is available to all throughout this world. Come journey together and spread positivity, as she takes you on a positive journey through her website alongside her books.

For more information about Ann Marie Ruby, any one of her books, or to read her blog posts and articles, subscribe to her website, www.annmarieruby.com.

Follow Ann Marie Ruby on social media:

Twitter: @AnnahMariahRuby
Facebook: @TheAnnMarieRuby
Instagram: @Ann_Marie_Ruby
Pinterest: @TheAnnMarieRuby

BOOKS BY THE AUTHOR

INSPIRATIONAL QUOTATIONS:

I have published four books of original inspirational quotations:

Spiritual Travelers:
Life's Journey From The Past
To The Present
For The Future

Spiritual
Messages:
From A Bottle

Spiritual Journey:
Life's Eternal Blessings

Spiritual
Inspirations:
Sacred Words
Of Wisdom

For all of you whom have requested my complete inspirational quotations, I have my complete ark of inspiration, I but call:

Spiritual Ark:
The Enchanted Journey Of Timeless
Quotations

219

THE SPIRITUAL SONGS COLLECTION:

When there was no hope, I found hope within these sacred words of prayers, I but call songs. Within this book, I have for you, 100 very sacred prayers:

Spiritual Songs:
Letters From My Chest

Prayers are but the sacred doors to an individual's enlightenment. This book has 123 prayers for all humans with humanity:

Spiritual Songs II:
Blessings From A Sacred
Soul

SPIRITUAL COLLECTION:

Do you believe in dreams? For within each individual dream, there is a hidden message and a miracle interlinked. Learn the spiritual, scientific, religious, and philosophical aspects of dreams. Walk with me as you travel through forty nights, through the pages of my book:

Spiritual Lighthouse:
The Dream Diaries Of Ann Marie Ruby

Humans have walked into an age where humanity now is being questioned as hate crimes have reached a catastrophic amount. Let us in union stop this crisis. Pick up my book and see if you too could join me in this fight:

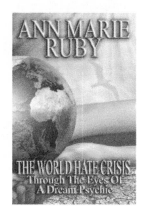

The World Hate Crisis:
Through The Eyes Of A Dream Psychic

Travel with me through the doors of birth, death, reincarnation, true soulmates, dreams, miracles, end of time, and the:

Eternal Truth:
The Tunnel Of Light

221

THE NETHERLANDS:

Oh the sacred travelers, be like the mystical river and journey through this blessed land through my book. Be the flying bird of wisdom and learn about a land I call, Heaven on Earth. For you the traveler, this is:

The Netherlands: Land Of My Dreams

Original poetry and hand-picked tales are bound together in this keepsake book. Come travel with me as I take you through the lives of the Dutch past. I call them:

Everblooming: Through The Twelve Provinces Of The Netherlands

Made in the USA
Las Vegas, NV
29 April 2023

71302296R00142